THE HUMAN BODY
How It Works

The Nervous System

THE HUMAN BODY
How It Works

THE HUMAN BODY
How It Works

The Nervous System

F. Fay Evans-Martin, Ph.D.

INTRODUCTION BY
Denton A. Cooley, M.D.
President and Surgeon-in-Chief
of the Texas Heart Institute
Clinical Professor of Surgery at the
University of Texas Medical School, Houston, Texas

CHELSEA HOUSE
PUBLISHERS
An imprint of Infobase Publishing

THE NERVOUS SYSTEM
Copyright © 2010 by Infobase Publishing

All rights reserved. No part of this book may be reproduced or utilized in any form
or by any means, electronic or mechanical, including photocopying, recording,
or by any information storage or retrieval systems, without permission in writing
from the publisher. For information, contact:

Chelsea House
An imprint of Infobase Publishing
132 West 31st Street
New York NY 10001

Library of Congress Cataloging-in-Publication Data
Evans-Martin, F. Fay.
  The nervous system / F. Fay Evans-Martin.
      p. cm.
  Includes bibliographical references and index.
  ISBN 978-1-60413-374-5 (hardcover)
  1. Nervous system. I. Title.

  QP355.2.E94 2009
  612.8—dc22   2009022141

Chelsea House books are available at special discounts when purchased in bulk
quantities for businesses, associations, institutions, or sales promotions. Please call
our Special Sales Department in New York at (212) 967-8800 or (800) 322-8755.

You can find Chelsea House on the World Wide Web at
http://www.chelseahouse.com

Text design by Erika Arroyo, Erik Lindstrom
Cover design by Takeshi Takahashi
Composition by EJB Publishing Services
Cover printed by Bang Printing, Brainerd, Minn.
Book printed and bound by Bang Printing, Brainerd, Minn.
Date printed: November, 2009
Printed in the United States of America

10 9 8 7 6 5 4 3 2 1

This book is printed on acid-free paper.

All links and Web addresses were checked and verified to be correct at the time of
publication. Because of the dynamic nature of the Web, some addresses and links may
have changed since publication and may no longer be valid.

Contents

Introduction

THE HUMAN BODY IS AN INCREDIBLY COMPLEX AND amazing structure. At best, it is a source of strength, beauty, and wonder. We can compare the healthy body to a well-designed machine whose parts work smoothly together. We can also compare it to a symphony orchestra in which each instrument has a different part to play. When all of the musicians play together, they produce beautiful music.

From a purely physical standpoint, our bodies are made mainly of water. We are also made of many minerals, including calcium, phosphorous, potassium, sulfur, sodium, chlorine, magnesium, and iron. In order of size, the elements of the body are organized into cells, tissues, and organs. Related organs are combined into systems, including the musculoskeletal, cardiovascular, nervous, respiratory, gastrointestinal, endocrine, and reproductive systems.

Our cells and tissues are constantly wearing out and being replaced without our even knowing it. In fact, much of the time, we take the body for granted. When it is working properly, we tend to ignore it. Although the heart beats about 100,000 times per day and we breathe more than 10 million times per year, we do not normally think about these things. When something goes wrong, however, our bodies tell us through pain and other symptoms. In fact, pain is a very effective alarm system that lets us know the body needs attention. If the pain does not go away, we may need to see a doctor. Even without medical help, the body has an amazing ability to heal itself. If we cut ourselves, the blood-clotting system works to seal the cut right away, and the immune defense system sends out special blood cells that are pro-grammed to heal the area.

During the past 50 years, doctors have gained the ability to repair or replace almost every part of the body. In my own field of cardiovascular surgery, we are able to open the heart and repair its valves, arteries, chambers, and connections. In many cases, these repairs can be done through a tiny "keyhole" incision that speeds up patient recovery and leaves hardly any scar. If the entire heart is diseased, we can replace it altogether, either with a donor heart or with a mechanical device. In the future, the use of mechanical hearts will probably be common in patients who would otherwise die of heart disease.

Until the mid-twentieth century, infections and contagious diseases related to viruses and bacteria were the most common causes of death. Even a simple scratch could become infected and lead to death from "blood poisoning." After penicillin and other antibiotics became available in the 1930s and 1940s, doc-tors were able to treat blood poisoning, tuberculosis, pneumo-nia, and many other bacterial diseases. Also, the introduction of modern vaccines allowed us to prevent childhood illnesses, smallpox, polio, flu, and other contagions that used to kill or cripple thousands.

Today, plagues such as the "Spanish flu" epidemic of 1918–19, which killed 20 to 40 million people worldwide, are unknown except in history books. Now that these diseases can be avoided, people are living long enough to have long-term (chronic) conditions such as cancer, heart failure, diabetes, and arthritis. Because chronic diseases tend to involve many organ systems or even the whole body, they cannot always be cured with surgery. These days, researchers are doing a lot of work at the cellular level, trying to find the underlying causes of chronic illnesses. Scientists recently finished mapping the human genome, which is a set of coded "instructions" programmed into our cells. Each cell contains 3 billion "letters" of this code. By showing how the body is made, the human genome will help researchers prevent and treat disease at its source, within the cells themselves.

The body's long-term health depends on many factors, called risk factors. Some risk factors, including our age, sex, and family history of certain diseases, are beyond our control. Other important risk factors include our lifestyle, behavior, and environment. Our modern lifestyle offers many advantages but is not always good for our bodies. In western Europe and the United States, we tend to be stressed, overweight, and out of shape. Many of us have unhealthy habits such as smoking cigarettes, abusing alcohol, or using drugs. Our air, water, and food often contain hazardous chemicals and industrial waste products. Fortunately, we can do something about most of these risk factors. At any age, the most important things we can do for our bodies are to eat right, exercise regularly, get enough sleep, and refuse to smoke, overuse alcohol, or use addictive drugs. We can also help clean up our environment. These simple steps will lower our chances of getting cancer, heart disease, or other serious disorders.

These days, thanks to the Internet and other forms of media coverage, people are more aware of health-related matters. The average person knows more about the human body than ever before. Patients want to understand their medical conditions and treatment options. They want to play a more active role, along with their doctors, in making medical decisions and in taking care of their own health.

I encourage you to learn as much as you can about your body and to treat your body well. These things may not seem too important to you now, while you are young, but the habits and behaviors that you practice today will affect your physical well-being for the rest of your life. The present book series, THE HUMAN BODY: HOW IT WORKS, is an excellent introduction to human biology and anatomy. I hope that it will awaken within you a lifelong interest in these subjects.

Denton A. Cooley, M.D.
President and Surgeon-in-Chief
of the Texas Heart Institute
Clinical Professor of Surgery at the
University of Texas Medical School, Houston, Texas

1

Our Amazing Nervous System

JOSHUA POKED AT THE EMBERS OF HIS CAMPFIRE AS HE STARED at the myriad of stars in the evening sky. The display of sunset colors had long faded from the sky, but the taste and aromas of his evening meal still lingered. Wildflowers filled the air with fragrance, and Joshua remembered noticing their beauty as he passed them during the day. A nearby stream trickled over the rocks, and the sounds of frogs and crickets filled the air. Rustling leaves and an occasional call from a night creature revealed the presence of forest animals.

Joshua nestled into his sleeping bag and soon fell asleep, dreaming of the natural wonders he had experienced that day. While Joshua slept, another natural wonder was actively at work, directing his dreams and regulating his breathing, his heartbeat, his body temperature, and the digestion of his evening meal. His amazing nervous system had received all the information he had observed during the day; interpreted it as beautiful sights, sounds, and aromas; and stored it for him to remember and enjoy. Every movement his body had made during his active day on the mountain trails had been under the control of his nervous system.

Protected within their bony casings of the skull and spinal column, the brain and spinal cord are the central core of the nervous system. A network of nerves branches out from them and acts as a fiber highway system for information coming from the environment and going to the muscles, glands, and body organs. Virtually every cell in the body is influenced by the nervous system. In turn, the nervous system is heavily affected by hormones and other chemicals produced by cells of the body.

NEURON THEORY

Beginning with the ancient Greek philosophers, there have been centuries of debate over the brain and its functions. It was not until the end of the nineteenth century that the structure and function of the nervous system began to become clear. Because nervous tissue is so soft, fragile, and complex, it was very difficult to study. Although scientists had observed and drawn nerve cells, they could not view all of their connections under a microscope.

In 1838, German botanist Matthias Jakob Schleiden introduced the theory that all plants are made up of individual units called cells. The next year, German physiologist Theodor Schwann introduced the theory that all animals are also made up of cells. Together, Schleiden's and Schwann's statements formed the basis of **cell theory**, which states that the cell is the basic unit of structure in all living organisms. Although cell theory quickly became popular, most scientists of the nineteenth century believed that the nervous system was a continuous network, or reticulum, of fibers, and was therefore an exception to cell theory. This concept about the organization of the nervous system became known as **reticular theory**.

A breakthrough came in 1873, when the Italian scientist Camillo Golgi reported his discovery of a special stain that made **neurons** (nerve cells) and their connections easier to study under a microscope. Because his technique was not refined enough to show the connections between individual neurons, Golgi continued to adhere to reticular theory. He believed the nervous system was a vast network of **cytoplasm** with many nuclei.

In 1886, Swiss anatomist Wilhelm His suggested that the neuron and its connections might, in fact, be an independent unit within the nervous system. Another Swiss scientist, August Forel, proposed a similar theory a few months later. Using Golgi's staining technique and improving upon it, Spanish scientist Santiago Ramón y Cajal showed in 1888 that the neuron and its connections were indeed an individual unit within the nervous system. In a paper published in 1891, German anatomist Wilhelm Waldeyer coined the term *neurone* and introduced the neuron doctrine. Known today as **neuron theory**, Waldeyer's concept extended cell theory to nervous tissue. However, it was not until after the invention of the electron microscope in the early 1930s that definitive evidence became available to show that neurons could communicate between themselves.

Golgi and Cajal were awarded a shared Nobel Prize in Physiology or Medicine in 1906 for their scientific studies of the nervous system. At the ceremony, each man gave a speech. Golgi's speech adhered to the reticular theory of nervous system structure. Cajal, on the other hand, spoke in enthusiastic support of neuron theory and gave evidence to contradict reticular theory. Since then, scientific studies have continued to support the neuron theory and have revealed more details that show how amazingly complex the nervous system really is. Although many questions remain to be answered, it is now clear that the nervous system is, in fact, made up of individual cells, just like the rest of the body.

NEURONS

The basic signaling unit of the nervous system is the neuron. Neurons are found in the brain, spinal cord, and throughout the body. Scientists estimate conservatively that there are more than 100 billion neurons in the brain and about 1 billion neurons in the spinal cord. Neurons come in many shapes and sizes and perform many different functions.

The number of different types of neurons may be as high as 10,000. Neurons are classified by either structure or function.

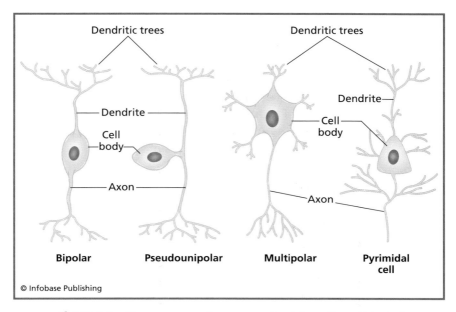

Figure 1.1   The processes of neurons extend from the cell body in three basic patterns. Unipolar neurons (not shown) have only one process, an axon, that has multiple terminal processes. Because there are no dendrites, the cell body receives incoming information. Bipolar neurons have an axon and a dendrite that arise from opposite ends of the cell body. The pseudounipolar neuron, a type of bipolar neuron, has one fused process that branches near the soma into an axon and a dendrite. Most central nervous system neurons are multipolar neurons, which have multiple dendritic trees and usually one axon. Pyramidal cells are a type of multipolar neuron.

Neurons can be divided into structural types based on the arrangement of their branches—the dendrites and axons. These structural types include **unipolar neurons**, **bipolar neurons**, **pseudounipolar neurons**, and **multipolar neurons** (Figure 1.1).

Functional types of neurons include sensory neurons, motor neurons, and interneurons. **Sensory neurons** generate nerve impulses in response to stimuli from the internal and external environments. These nerve impulses are transmitted to the brain, where they are interpreted. **Motor neurons** send impulses from the brain and spinal cord to the muscles and glands, resulting in movements and glandular secretions. **Interneurons** relay information between two other neurons, to which they are connected.

Like other cells, the **cell body**, or **soma**, of a neuron has an outer plasma membrane, or **cell membrane**, that encloses the watery cytoplasm in which the cell **nucleus** (plural: *nuclei*) and a variety of **organelles** are found (Figure 1.2). The nucleus is the control center of the cell. It directs the activities of the other organelles, which are responsible for all of the cell's functions. Unlike most other cells, neurons do not divide to reproduce themselves. Also unlike most other cells, neurons are able to transmit an electrochemical signal.

Most cells in the body have geometric shapes—they are squarish, cubical, or spherical. Neurons, on the other hand, are irregular in shape and have a number of spiderlike extensions, or "processes," from the cell body. The neuron's processes send and receive information to and from other neurons.

In most neurons, extending from one end of the cell body are short processes called **dendrites** that branch in a treelike manner. In fact, their arrangement is referred to as the "dendritic tree." A single neuron can have anywhere from 1 to 20 dendrites, each of which can branch many times. Dendrites receive messages from other neurons and carry them toward the cell body.

Dendritic spines are short, thornlike structures that appear on the dendrites. There may be thousands of dendritic spines on the dendrites of just one neuron. This greatly increases the surface area that the dendritic tree has available for receiving signals from other neurons. Together, these structures receive information from as many as 10,000 other neurons.

Each neuron generally has one **axon**, which extends from the cell body at the end that is opposite the dendrites. Axons carry messages away from the cell body. Although the cell body is usually just 5 to 100 micrometers, or µm, (0.0002 to 0.0004

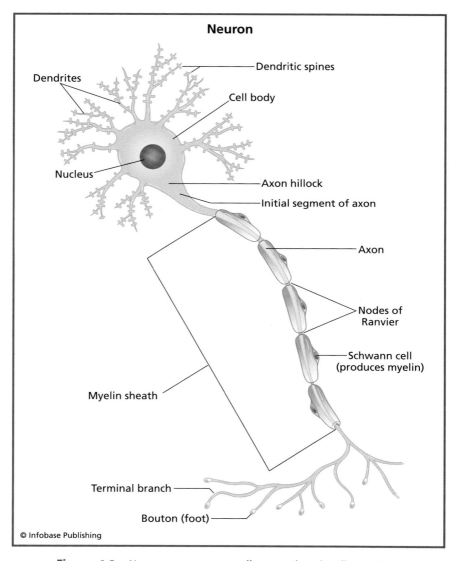

Figure 1.2 Neurons, or nerve cells, are the signaling units of the nervous system. The myelin sheath, composed of Schwann cell processes in peripheral neurons and processes of oligodendrocytes in central neurons, insulates the axon and helps the electrical impulses travel faster. The gaps in the myelin between these processes are called nodes of Ranvier.

inches) in diameter, axons can range in length from 1 millimeter to as much as 1 meter (0.04 in). Some axons, especially the longer ones, are myelinated—covered with a fatty substance known as **myelin**. This covering forms what is called a myelin sheath. Sometimes axons branch into one or more *collateral axons*, each of which ends in several small branches known as *axon terminals*. To relay messages, axons from other neurons contact the dendritic spines, and the cell bodies of other neurons. Axons can end on other axons, on a muscle, on a tiny blood vessel, or in the **extracellular fluid** that bathes the cells of the body. A dendrite can also connect to another dendrite to communicate with it.

Many chemicals called **neurotransmitters** are synthesized and stored in the axon terminals. Some are synthesized in the cell body and transported down the axon to the terminals. When released from the axon terminal, neurotransmitters carry chemical messages to other neurons, to muscle fibers, and to organs and glands. Neurotransmitters trigger nerve impulses, stimulate muscle contraction, and affect the functions of organs and glands of the body systems.

THE SYNAPSE

How does a nerve signal travel from one neuron to another? Between the tip of each axon terminal and the point on the target neuron (usually a dendritic spine or the cell body) to which the axon sends a nerve signal, there is a tiny gap. It measures about 10 to 20 nanometers (3.94 to 7.87 in) across and is called the synaptic cleft. The term **synapse** refers to the synaptic cleft and the areas on the two neurons that are involved in the transmission and reception of a chemical signal. The *presynaptic neuron* is the one that sends the message. It releases a neurotransmitter into the synaptic cleft. Every neuron produces one or more kinds of neurotransmitters and stores them inside spherical structures called synaptic vesicles located in the axon terminal. When a nerve signal travels down the axon and arrives at the axon terminal, the synaptic vesicles move to the presynaptic membrane, bind to it, and release their contents into the synaptic cleft. Neurotransmitters diffuse across the synaptic cleft and bind to a neurotransmitter-specific receptor, a membrane protein, found on the surface of the plasma membrane of the *postsynaptic* (receiving) *neuron* (Figure 1.3). A neurotransmitter molecule fits into its receptor protein like a key in a lock and causes an ion channel to open.

GLIA

Glia are special cells that play a supporting role in the nervous system. They outnumber neurons by about 10 to 1 in the brain, where they make up at least half of the brain's volume. The number of glia in other parts of the nervous system has

THE BLOOD-BRAIN BARRIER

Astrocytes also contribute to the formation of the **blood-brain barrier**. Processes from astrocytes called "end feet" adhere to the blood vessels of the brain and secrete chemical signals that induce (cause) the formation of tight junctions between the endothelial cells that line the blood vessels. As a result, substances from the extracellular fluid cannot move easily into these cells. The small pores called fenestrations and some of the transport mechanisms that are present in peripheral blood vessels are absent in the membranes of the cells that line the brain's blood vessels.

The blood-brain barrier keeps most substances other than oxygen, glucose, and essential amino acids from entering the brain from the bloodstream. It protects the brain from toxins, peripheral neurotransmitters, and other substances that would interfere with the brain's functioning. Most large molecules cannot cross this blood-brain barrier. Small fat-soluble molecules and uncharged particles such as carbon dioxide and oxygen, however, diffuse easily across this barrier. Glucose and essential amino acids are transported across by special transporter proteins. Toxins that can diffuse across the blood-brain barrier include nerve gases, alcohol, and nicotine.

not yet been determined. Unlike neurons, glia are replaced constantly throughout life. Like neurons, glia have many extensions coming off their cell bodies. Unlike neurons, however, most glia do not transmit electrical impulses. A recent discovery—that a subtype of **oligodendrocyte** precursor cells (OPSs) generate electrical signals—challenges the traditional view that no glial cells can do so. These special glial cells not only generate electrical impulses but also receive input from neuronal axons.

There are four main types of glial cells: **astrocytes**; myelin-producing oligodendrocytes and **Schwann cells**; **ependymal cells**; and **microglia**. Astrocytes surround neurons and provide structural support to hold neurons in place. They provide nutritional support by contacting nearby blood vessels and transporting glucose and other nutrients from the bloodstream. Among the other functions they perform are the uptake of neurotransmitters from the synapse, regulation of the extracellular potassium (K^+) concentration, synthesis and release of nerve growth factors, and the scavenging of dead cells after an injury to the brain.

Oligodendrocytes are found in the brain and spinal cord, whereas Schwann cells are found in the **peripheral nervous system**. Both cell types have fewer extensions than astrocytes. Their main function is to provide the myelin sheath that covers myelinated axons. Like astrocytes, they also help bring nutritional support to neurons. Schwann cells secrete growth factors that help repair damaged nerves outside the brain and spinal cord.

Myelin is the covering of glial extensions that wrap around the axon of a neuron in as many as 100 layers. Each oligodendrocyte may wrap a different process around one segment of the axon of up to 50 different neurons. In the nerves outside the brain and spinal cord, Schwann cell processes wrap around one short segment of the axon of just one neuron. The layers of myelin provide additional electrical insulation that helps the nerve signal travel faster and farther. Each wrap of a glial process around the axon provides two additional lipid bilayers from which the cytoplasm has been squeezed out in the wrapping process. Myelinated neurons have the additional electrical insulation provided by the layers of myelin. An unmyelinated axon has only the lipid bilayer of its own plasma membrane for electrical insulation.

Ependymal cells are glial cells that line the **ventricles**, the fluid-filled cavities of the brain. Unlike other glial cells, they do not have processes coming off the cell body. They secrete cerebrospinal fluid, the liquid that fills the ventricles and the spinal canal. Cerebrospinal fluid acts as a shock-absorbing cushion to protect the brain from blows to the head. In effect, this fluid makes the brain float inside the skull. The cerebrospinal fluid also removes waste products from the brain.

The **ventricular system** is the continuous system of ventricles in the brain through which the cerebrospinal fluid circulates. It consists of the paired lateral ventricles in the **cerebrum**, the third ventricle in the **diencephalon**, the cerebral aqueduct in the midbrain, and the fourth ventricle between the **cerebellum** and the **pons** and **medulla**. Cerebrospinal fluid leaves the fourth ventricle through several small openings and bathes the brain and spinal cord. The spinal canal runs through the center of the spinal cord and is continuous with the ventricular system of the brain.

Small cells called microglia migrate from the blood into the brain. They act as the cleanup crew when nerve cells die. They also produce chemicals called growth factors that help damaged neurons to heal. When you view a damaged area of the brain under a microscope, you can see glial cells clustered in the places where dead cells were removed.

THE PLASMA MEMBRANE
AND THE MEMBRANE POTENTIAL

The plasma membrane of neurons is made up of a lipid bilayer, a double layer of fatty molecules. Phospholipids are the most common lipid found in the cell membrane. Because the phosphate-containing "head" of a phospholipid molecule

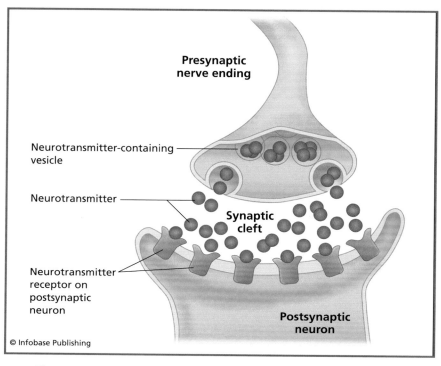

© Infobase Publishing

Figure 1.3   The synapse is the junction of a neuron with another neuron or a muscle fiber. The synaptic cleft is the tiny space between the axon ending of one neuron and the cell with which it communicates. Neurotransmitters carry the nerve signal as a chemical message across the synaptic cleft from the first (presynaptic) neuron to the second (postsynaptic) neuron. The neurotransmitter molecules bind to receptors in the membrane of the postsynaptic neuron.

is attracted to water (hydrophilic) and the fatty acid-containing "tail" is repelled by water (hydrophobic), the phospholipid molecules spontaneously form a bilayer with the fatty acid tails in the middle (Figure 1.4). This bilayer forms a barrier between the water outside the cell and the water inside the cell. It also keeps substances that are dissolved in water, such as ions, from crossing the cell membrane. Very few substances other than gases can cross the lipid bilayer easily.

Wedged between the fatty molecules of the plasma membrane are many proteins. Some of these proteins have pores, or

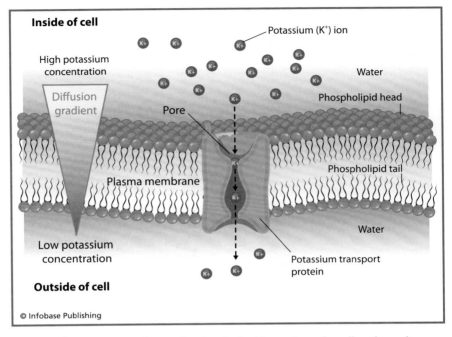

Inside of cell

Potassium (K⁺) ion

High potassium
concentration

Water

Diffusion
gradient

Pore

Phospholipid head

Plasma membrane

Phospholipid tail

Water

Low potassium
concentration

Potassium transport
protein

Outside of cell

© Infobase Publishing

Figure 1.4   Few ions and molecules besides water and small uncharged
molecules, such as oxygen and carbon dioxide, can easily pass through
the lipid bilayer of the cell membrane. Other substances needed for
cell function must cross the cell membrane through special transporter
proteins that span the lipid bilayer. These transporter proteins are highly
selective, allowing only a particular ion or molecule to pass.

channels, that let certain ions enter the cell. Some channels are
open all the time to let particular ions move back and forth.
These channels are said to be *ungated*. Other channels stay
closed unless they get a signal that causes them to open. These
are referred to as *gated* channels.

Protein molecules, which are kept inside the neuron,
have a negative charge. As a result, they give the entire cell
interior a negative charge as compared with the extracellular
fluid. The concentration of certain ions differs between the
inside of the cell and the extracellular fluid surrounding the
cell. The interior of the cell has a higher concentration of
K⁺ ions, whereas the extracellular fluid has higher concen-

trations of sodium (Na⁺) and chloride (Cl⁻) ions. A special membrane protein, known as the sodium-potassium pump, helps control the Na^+ and K^+ concentrations by using energy to pump three Na^+ ions out for every two K^+ ions it allows in. The area just inside of the plasma membrane is about 70 millivolts, or mV (a millivolt is one thousandth of a volt), more negative than that of the extracellular fluid just outside the cell membrane. This electrical charge is called the resting potential of the membrane. The interior of the cell membrane is said to be "polarized."

THE ACTION POTENTIAL

Unlike other cells, excitable cells such as neurons can generate an electrical current called an **action potential**. As Na+ ions enter the postsynaptic neuron through ion channels activated by neurotransmitters, tiny electrical currents are produced. These currents travel to the **axon hillock**, the area where the cell body ends and the axon begins. There, the tiny electrical currents sum together. Each neuron receives thousands of neural signals per second from other neurons. Some of them are excitatory and open Na^+ channels. Others are inhibitory and open Cl^- or K^+ channels. Depending on the number and type of tiny electrical currents generated as the neurotransmitter chemicals bind to the receptors on the postsynaptic membrane, the axon hillock gets a message to fire or not to fire an action potential. It fires an action potential only if there are enough currents to open a large enough number of voltage-gated Na^+ channels to make the membrane over the axon hillock reach its threshold potential.

When the sum of these tiny currents pushes the membrane potential of the axon hillock down by about 20 mV—to what is called the *threshold potential*—there is a sudden, dramatic change in the voltage difference across the membrane. At this point, when voltage on the inside of the membrane is 50 mV more negative than that on the outside, the interior voltage makes a sudden reversal that continues until the voltage inside the membrane is 30 mV more *positive* than that outside the membrane.

This sudden reversal in voltage is the action potential. It lasts for about 1 millisecond. During this time, Na$^+$ ions pour into the cell through voltage-gated ion channels. The change in voltage lets K$^+$ ions leave the cell more freely, causing a loss of positive charge and leading to a sudden reversal of the voltage inside the membrane back to a level that is slightly more negative than the resting potential (Figure 1.5). The drop in voltage below that of the resting potential is called **hyperpolarization**. As K$^+$ ions begin to reenter the cell, the voltage inside the membrane slowly returns to the resting potential.

The reason that the action potential travels in only one direction down the axon is because there is a **refractory period** that begins immediately after the firing of an action potential. During the millisecond in which the action potential is firing, the neuron cannot fire again because the Na$^+$ channels have been been left inactive after opening. This period is called the absolute refractory period. As the influx of K$^+$ ions pushes the voltage downward to below the threshold potential and Na$^+$ channels begin to reactivate, a relative refractory period occurs, which overlaps with the period of hyperpolarization. During this phase, the neuron can fire an action potential, but a greater depolarization than usual is needed for it to do so.

As the action potential travels down an unmyelinated axon away from the cell body, it causes the voltage of the area near the axon membrane to be more positive. In turn, this opens more voltage-gated ion channels. As the voltage of the adjoining intracellular membrane drops to its threshold potential, another action potential fires. This process continues until a series of action potentials travels the length of the axon.

In myelinated axons, the extra insulation lets nerve impulses travel very fast—up to 120 m/s (394 feet/s), which is more than the length of a football field. The extra insulation

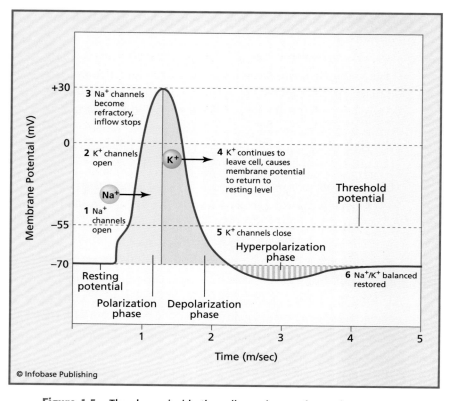

Figure 1.5 The charge inside the cell membrane of a resting neuron is -70 mV. During the depolarization phase of the action potential, Na⁺ ions pour into the neuron. During the repolarization phase, K⁺ ions flow out of the cell. The hyperpolarization phase results from an excess of potassium ions leaving the cell.

provided by the myelin sheath also allows an action potential to travel much farther in a myelinated axon. Each myelinated segment measures about 0.1 to 0.5 μm (0.000004 to 0.000020 in.) in length. Between these segments are tiny unmyelinated gaps called the **nodes of Ranvier**. At these nodes, Na⁺ ions enter through voltage-gated ion channels to propagate, or reproduce, the action potential. As a new action potential is generated at each node of Ranvier, the neural signal appears to "jump" from one node to the next.

CONNECTIONS

The nervous system is an intricate network of neurons (nerve cells) and their connections. Surrounding the neurons are glia, which play many supportive roles in the nervous system. Neurons receive and process chemical messages from other neurons and then send electrical signals down their axons to trigger the release of neurotransmitters—chemical messengers—that go out to other neurons. The electrical current that travels down the neuronal axon is made up of a series of action potentials, which are generated by the opening of voltage-gated Na^+ channels in the axon membrane.

2

Development of the Nervous System

THE FIRST VISIBLE SIGNS OF THE DEVELOPING NERVOUS SYSTEM show up during the third week after fertilization. At this point, the embryo consists of three layers of cells: an outer layer called the *ectoderm*, a middle layer called the *mesoderm*, and an inner layer called the *endoderm*. The ectoderm develops into the nervous system, as well as the hair, skin, and nails—outer structures that cover the body. The mesoderm develops into muscle, bone, and connective tissue, as well as some of the internal organs, including the heart and blood vessels. The endoderm develops into the digestive and respiratory tracts and additional internal organs.

Around day 16 of development, a thickened layer of cells, called the neural plate, appears in the midline of the **dorsal** surface of the ectodermal layer. Because we walk upright, the term *dorsal* corresponds to the **posterior**, or back, side in human beings. The term **ventral** refers to the opposite, or **anterior**, surface—the front side (Figure 2.1).

As the neural plate develops, the cells at its edges multiply faster than the rest. This makes the plate's edges curve upward to form a neural groove in the center. By day 21 of development, the edges of the two sides of the neural plate meet and

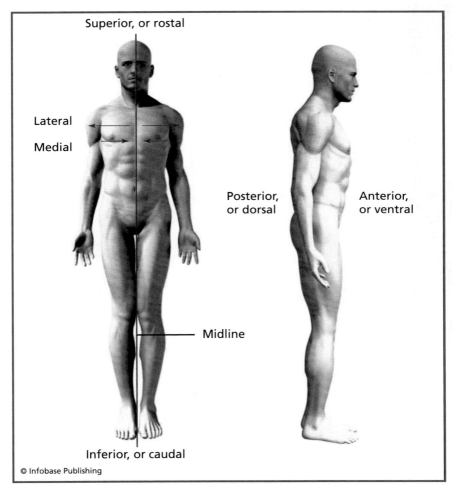

Figure 2.1   The directional terms that describe relative positions in the body include posterior and anterior, dorsal and ventral, lateral and medial, and superior and inferior.

join to form the **neural tube**. This fusion begins at the place where the neck region will eventually be located. It then continues to join rostrally (toward the head end) and caudally (toward the tail end) until the whole dorsal surface of the tube is fused. Finally, the **rostral** and **caudal** ends of the neural tube close on day 24 and day 26, respectively. This process

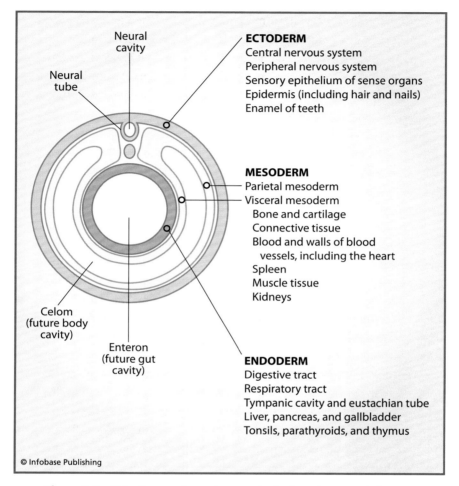

Neural
cavity

Neural
tube

ECTODERM
Central nervous system
Peripheral nervous system
Sensory epithelium of sense organs
Epidermis (including hair and nails)
Enamel of teeth

MESODERM
Parietal mesoderm
Visceral mesoderm
  Bone and cartilage
  Connective tissue
  Blood and walls of blood
    vessels, including the heart
  Spleen
  Muscle tissue
  Kidneys

Celom
(future body
cavity)

Enteron
(future gut
cavity)

ENDODERM
Digestive tract
Respiratory tract
Tympanic cavity and eustachian tube
Liver, pancreas, and gallbladder
Tonsils, parathyroids, and thymus

© Infobase Publishing

Figure 2.2   This diagram shows the neural tube just after neurulation. Notice that the primary germ layers—the ectoderm, endoderm, and mesoderm—are still present. Each layer gives rise to a specific set of structures in the developing body.

of forming the neural tube is known as *primary neurulation* (Figure 2.2).

The adult spinal cord can be divided into five regions, from the neck down: cervical, thoracic, lumbar, sacral, and coccygeal. The cervical, thoracic, and lumbar segments of the

spinal cord develop from the neural tube. The sacral and coccygeal segments, however, develop from the caudal eminence,
a cell mass located caudal to the neural tube. It appears around
day 20, grows larger, and then forms a cavity before it joins
the neural tube. This process, called *secondary neurulation*, is
completed by day 42.

As the neural tube closes, cells separate from the upper
edges, or crests, of the neural folds to form the *neural crest*.
From the neural crest, parts of the **peripheral nervous system**
will develop. The peripheral nervous system includes all the
nerves and neurons outside the brain and spinal cord. Cells
from the neural crest move to a position on either side of the
neural tube. The neural crest cells give rise to sensory neurons, the **adrenal medulla**, neurons and glia of the autonomic
division of the peripheral nervous system, as well as two
inner layers of the **meninges**, membranes that cover the brain
and spinal cord. The outer layer of the meninges develops
from the mesoderm.

As the neural tube fuses, it separates from the ectodermal
layer to become enclosed inside the body. The neural tube now
develops into the structures of the central nervous system. Its
central cavity develops into the ventricular system of the brain,
which is continuous with the spinal canal. Precursor cells for
the neurons and glia that will populate the developing nervous
system originate from the ventricular layer, which lines the
inner surface of the neural tube. Developing neurons migrate
from the ventricular zone to their final destinations by using
the processes of astrocytes called radial glia as a supportive
scaffold. Once they reach their destinations, the migrated
neurons send out processes and form synaptic connections
with other neurons and with muscle cells. Failure of neurons
to reach their proper destination can result in birth defects and
loss of function.

By the sixth week after conception, the nervous system has
developed to its basic form. The major structures are all recognizable by the tenth week. All brain structures are present in

an immature form by the end of the first trimester (first three months) of development. Neuronal proliferation and migration is greatest during the second trimester and continues until the time of birth. Myelination of axons is greatest during the third trimester but continues to take place until adulthood. The development and reorganization of synaptic connections between neurons occur throughout life.

During the first three months of fetal development, the vertebral column and spinal cord grow at about the same rate. The nerves from the spinal cord exit directly through openings in the vertebral column called **intervertebral foramina**. After this point, however, the vertebral column grows faster than the spinal cord. This leaves a space called the **lumbar cistern** in the lower part of the vertebral canal that is not filled by the spinal cord. Spinal nerves associated with the foramina in the area of the lumbar cistern travel down from their origin in the spinal cord through the lumbar cistern before they leave through their associated foramina. It is from the lumbar cistern that cerebrospinal fluid is withdrawn in a diagnostic procedure called the spinal tap.

At birth, the brain weighs 400 grams (0.88 lbs) on average. By age three, the weight of the brain has tripled due to myelination of axons and development of neuronal processes and synaptic connections. By the time a person is 11 years old, the brain has reached its maximum weight, which can vary from 1,100 to 1,700 g (2.4 to 3.7 lbs). The average human brain weighs about 1,400 g (3.1 lbs). After age 50, people experience a gradual decrease in brain weight, which may cause a slow decline in some cognitive, or thinking, functions.

DEVELOPMENTAL NEUROLOGICAL DISORDERS

Approximately 40% of all infant deaths before the first birthday happen because something goes wrong with the development of the central nervous system. A leading cause of death shortly after birth is neural tube defects. In fact, problems with neural tube development are the leading cause of infant deaths (second only to heart defects). If the neural tube does not close properly, the nervous system may not be correctly formed. This occurs in about 1 out of every 1,000 live births. Most fetuses with major nervous system malformations die before or within the first year after birth.

Spina bifida is a birth defect that results when the neural tube does not close completely at the caudal (tail) end. Depending on how severe the condition is, the overlying vertebrae and tissue may not develop, which lets the meninges and spinal cord protrude to the surface of the back. Spina bifida may also cause varying degrees of leg paralysis and problems with bladder control. Supplementing the diets of pregnant women with folic acid has been found to reduce neural tube defects.

WHAT IS NEUROGENESIS?

Scientists once thought that a human infant was born with all the neurons it would ever have and that no new neurons were produced after birth. You can imagine the ripples in the scientific world in 1998 when Peter S. Eriksson, Fred H. Gage, and their colleagues announced their discovery of **neurogenesis**—the production of new neurons in the adult brain. These scientists injected bromodeoxyuridine, which is incorporated into newly formed DNA, into terminally ill patients and examined their brains after they died. They found neurons in the hippocampus that were stained by this molecular marker, which indicated that they had been produced after the injection. Later research has also detected the migration of stem cells from the subventricular zone (SVZ) to sites in the **cerebral cortex**. The SVZ is a layer of cells that lies underneath the ependymal layer in the walls of the lateral ventricles. Related studies in rodents have shown that exercise, enriched environments, and learning enhance neurogenesis and that stress and inflammation reduce it. Scientists hope that neurogenesis research will eventually yield answers that will help restore or regenerate brains afflicted with neurodegenerative disease.

Therefore, physicians now recommend 400 micrograms of folic acid per day during pregnancy and for all female patients anticipating having children.

Anencephaly is a birth defect that can result when the rostral (head) end of the neural tube does not close all the way. When this happens, the cerebral hemispheres will be partially absent, and some of the overlying bone and tissue may not form as well. When a baby is born with this condition, it is usually blind, deaf, and unconscious. It may also have no ability to feel pain. Infants with anencephaly almost always die within hours—or, at most, days—after they are born.

Chromosomal abnormalities can cause problems in brain development. One example is *Down syndrome,* which occurs in 1 out of 700 infants. The children of mothers who are over age 45 at the time of birth are more likely to suffer from Down syndrome—the chances are 1 in 25 as compared with 1 in 1,550 for mothers under the age of 20. Babies born with Down syndrome have an extra copy of chromosome 21. Because of this, the disorder is sometimes called trisomy 21. Symptoms of Down syndrome differ between individuals but can include mental retardation, flattened facial features, and short stature. Early interventions, including nutritional and other therapies, are now allowing children with Down syndrome to develop more normally and live longer, healthier lives.

Fragile X syndrome is an inherited developmental disorder that results from a mutant gene on the X chromosome. Symptoms include mental retardation, an elongated face with a large jaw, enlarged testes (in males), and flared ears.

Other developmental abnormalities can result from malnutrition or from exposure to radiation, environmental toxins, drugs, and some pathogens (organisms that cause infections). Viruses (such as rubella and cytomegalovirus), bacteria (such as the spirochete bacterium that causes syphilis), and protozoans (such as *Toxoplasma,* which is found in garden dirt and cat feces) can all lead to nervous system defects. Drugs used to treat epilepsy can cause defective neural tube development.

Neonatal exposure to lead or mercury can lead to neurological problems. Smoking, drinking alcohol, or taking cocaine or other drugs of abuse during pregnancy can also cause problems in the fetus's neurological development. There is evidence that cocaine, for example, interferes with the myelination of axons in adults.

Because there is an intimate relationship between the nervous system and the structures of the skin, bone, muscles, and meninges, a person who has a defect in his or her nervous system development usually has problems in other areas as well. Defects in facial features often accompany problems in brain development. This is particularly true in cases of *fetal alcohol syndrome*, which can occur if the mother drinks alcohol while she is pregnant. Children with fetal alcohol syndrome often have slitlike eyes, a thin upper lip, and a small face. They may also have behavioral and cognitive problems as well as other birth defects, such as hearing impairments, heart defects, and speech impediments.

CONNECTIONS

The nervous system starts to develop during the third week after conception. The neural plate appears first, then folds upward to form the neural tube. Neural crest cells separate from the neural tube as it closes to form what will become the peripheral nervous system. By the fifth week, the five major areas of the brain have developed as pouches that come off the neural tube. As the walls of the neural tube thicken and form the future brain structures, the cavity of the neural tube grows into the ventricular system of the brain. Neurons that will make up the brain structures move from the inner lining of the neural cavity to their final destinations. Ten weeks after conception, all the major brain structures are recognizable. It was once thought that at birth, a person already had all the

(continues)

(continued)

neurons that he or she would have for a lifetime. However, recent discoveries of the formation of new neurons (neurogenesis) in the adult human brain have changed that assmption. Myelination also continues to occur into adulthood. Synaptic changes take place throughout life as well. Problems with the closure of the neural tube or in the migration of neurons result in birth defects. Injury or exposure to toxins can also cause developmental disorders in the growing nervous system.

3

Organization of the Nervous System

THE COMPLEXITY OF THE HUMAN NERVOUS SYSTEM, particularly the brain, is such that the most sophisticated computers have been unable to match it. Every moment of the day, nerve signals are speeding along pathways between the various components of the nervous system. We are unaware of much of this activity, which automatically regulates the vital functions and rhythms of our bodies. Neural signals along other pathways bring us information about our environment. The nervous system processes this information and stores it for future use. Nervous system activity also enables us to respond to and manipulate our environment. Communication and thinking are made possible by the synchronization of many neural messages. Let's take a look at how the brain and the rest of the nervous system work together to make all of this possible.

DIVISIONS OF THE NERVOUS SYSTEM

The two main divisions of the nervous system are the **central nervous system (CNS)** and the peripheral nervous system (Figure 3.1). Table 3.1 shows how the central and peripheral nervous systems are organized. The central nervous system

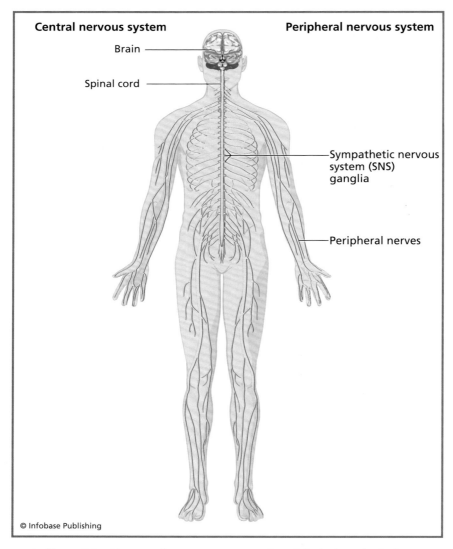

Figure 3.1   The central nervous system consists of the brain and spinal cord, whereas the sensory and ganglionic neurons and the peripheral nerves make up the peripheral nervous system. The sympathetic nervous system ganglia actually form a chain (not visible here) near the spinal cord, while the cell bodies of sensory neurons that lead to the spinal cord are located in clusters (called ganglia) next to the spinal cord.

consists of the brain and spinal cord, which lie within the bones of the skull and vertebral column. The peripheral nervous system includes all the components of the nervous system that lie outside the brain and spinal cord. Axons from neurons in the brain travel down the spinal cord and out to their targets. These axons travel in bundles within fiber tracts (pathways) down the spinal cord and then travel out to their targets through the peripheral nerves. Sensory fibers from different parts of the body travel in the opposite direction through the peripheral nerves to the spinal cord and up to their targets in the brain.

THE CENTRAL NERVOUS SYSTEM: THE BRAIN

The major divisions of the brain are the cerebrum, diencephalon, brainstem, and cerebellum (Figure 3.2).

TABLE 3.1: DIVISIONS OF THE NERVOUS SYSTEM

CENTRAL NERVOUS SYSTEM	FUNCTION
Brain	Control center
Spinal cord	Central relay center
PERIPHERAL NERVOUS SYSTEM	
Somatic nervous system	
Sensory nerves	Transduction
Motor nerves	Carry motor commands
Autonomic nervous system	
Parasympathetic nervous system	Maintain homeostasis
Sympathetic nervous system	Stress response
Enteric nervous system	Digestion

The Cerebrum

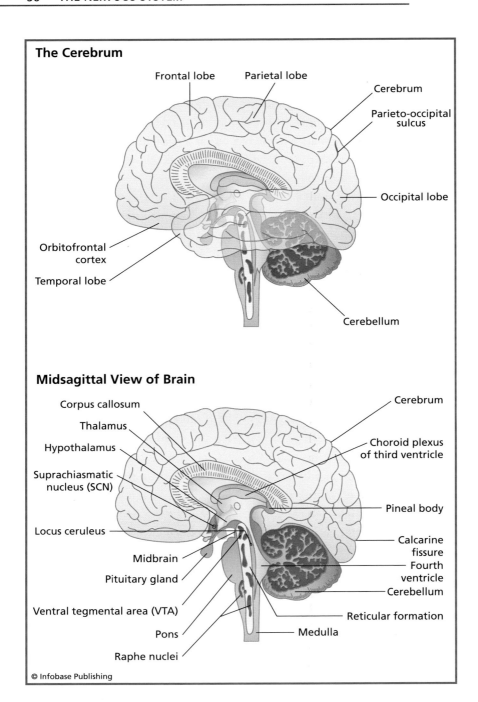

Frontal lobe

Parietal lobe

Cerebrum

Parieto-occipital sulcus

Occipital lobe

Orbitofrontal cortex

Temporal lobe

Cerebellum

Midsagittal View of Brain

Corpus callosum

Thalamus

Hypothalamus

Suprachiasmatic nucleus (SCN)

Locus ceruleus

Midbrain

Pituitary gland

Ventral tegmental area (VTA)

Pons

Raphe nuclei

Cerebrum

Choroid plexus of third ventricle

Pineal body

Calcarine fissure

Fourth ventricle

Cerebellum

Reticular formation

Medulla

© Infobase Publishing

The Cerebrum

The two halves of the cerebrum, or the *cerebral hemispheres*, form the largest portion of the brain. Each hemisphere is covered by the cerebral cortex a thin layer of **gray matter** that is about 3 mm (0.12 in) deep. (*Cortex* means "bark" or "rind.") Gray matter is the term used to describe areas where the neurons are densest and their cell bodies give the brain a grayish-brown color.

The cerebral cortex contains ridges (*gyri*) and fissures (*sulci*) that make it look something like a crumpled piece of paper. Underneath the cerebral cortex is a much deeper layer of fiber tracts with axons that travel to and from the cortex. It has a whitish appearance due to the myelin in the axons. Areas of the brain where fiber tracts predominate are called **white matter**. Large fiber tracts that connect areas of gray matter in the brain and that surround the central region of gray matter in the spinal cord are also part of the white matter.

In each hemisphere, the cerebral cortex is divided into four lobes by deep fissures, or grooves, called sulci. The central sulcus crosses the cortex horizontally and extends down to the lateral sulcus, which defines the upper limit of the **temporal lobe**. Above the temporal lobe and in front of (rostral to) the central sulcus is the **frontal lobe**. Behind (caudal to) the frontal lobe and bounded on the rear by the **parieto-occipital sulcus** (the fissure separating the occipital and parietal lobes) is the **parietal lobe**. The **occipital lobe** surrounds the posterior pole (center back) of the cerebral cortex and is bounded at the

Figure 3.2 (*opposite page*) (Top) The major divisions of the brain include the cerebrum, cerebellum, brainstem, and diencephalon. The cerebrum includes the frontal, parietal, occipital, and temporal lobes. (Bottom) This midsagittal view is how the brain would look if it were cut down the the middle between the two cerebral hemispheres. The corpus callosum is the fiber bundle that connects the two hemispheres and allows them to exchange information. Most structures of the brain are paired—there is one on each side of the brain.

front by the parieto-occipital sulcus and an imaginary line that goes from the edge of the parieto-occipital sulcus down to the occipital notch. An imaginary line that runs from the edge of the lateral sulcus to intersect at right angles with this line marks the lower boundary of the parietal lobe.

The frontal lobe controls thinking, speech, emotion, and the production and planning of movements. The occipital lobe receives and interprets visual input from the eyes as vision. The parietal lobe receives sensory messages from the skin, joints, and muscles and interprets them as pain, touch, and the position of the arms and legs in space. Auditory (hearing) and visual inputs are also integrated with the **somatosensory input** in the parietal lobe. Primary auditory input goes to the temporal lobe, which interprets it as sound. The temporal lobe also plays a role in feeling emotion, perceiving form and color, and understanding speech. In addition, the temporal lobe houses areas to which the olfactory tract "projects," or travels to, after it crosses the ventral surface of the brain.

Six layers of neurons in the cerebral cortex send and receive messages through an extensive network of axons, called the *corona radiatus,* that fan out under the cortex. These axons come together into fiber tracts that descend toward the brainstem. Fibers connecting the two cerebral hemispheres form a dense structure called the **corpus callosum** that arches above the lateral ventricles. Extensive communication occurs between the two cerebral hemispheres, particularly between paired structures (one in each hemisphere). Table 3.2 shows the different structures of the brain and how they are organized.

Deep in the cerebral hemispheres are several important nuclei (Figure 3.2). (A group of neurons with similar functions is referred to as a nucleus when it is located in the central nervous system, and as a **ganglion** when it is located in the peripheral nervous system.) In the temporal lobe, the **hippocampus** is important in processing emotions and memories. In front of the anterior tip of the hippocampus is the **amygdala**, which helps us express emotion and generate a response to stressful events. The **basal ganglia** are important in the control of movement.

TABLE 3.2 ANATOMICAL DIVISIONS AND STRUCTURES OF THE BRAIN

Division	Ventricle	Subdivision	Major Structures
Forebrain	Lateral	Telencephalon	Cerebral cortex Basal ganglia Amygdala Hippocampus Septal nuclei
	Third	Diencephalon	Thalamus Hypothalamus

Midbrain	Cerebral aqueduct	Mesencephalon	Tectum (roof):
			   Superior collicui
			   Inferior colliculi
			
			Cerebral peduncles
			
			Tegmentum (floor):
			   Rostral reticular formation
			   Periaqueductal gray matter
			   Red nucleus
			   Ventral tegmental area
			   Substantia nigra
			   Locus coeruleus nuclei
			   Cranial nerve nuclei
			   (CNN) III, IV, V

Hindbrain	Fourth	Metencephalon	Cerebellum
			
			Pons:
			   Reticular formation
			   Raphe nuclei
			   CNN V, VI, VII, VIII

		Myelencephalon	Medulla oblongata:
			   Reticular formation
			   Raphe nuclei
			   CNN V, VII, VIII, IX, X, XII

* The spinal trigeminal nucleus extends into the caudal pons from the dorsal column of the spinal cord with which it is continuous. The nucleus of cranial nerve XI, which exits from the medulla, is located just below the junction of the medulla and the spinal cord.

They are centrally located in the brain, just above and to the side of the **thalamus** (see Figure 5.3). One of the basal ganglia is a C-shaped structure called the **caudate nucleus**.

The Diencephalon

Beneath the cerebral hemispheres and on either side of the third ventricle are paired groups of nuclei called the thalamus and **hypothalamus,** which together are known as the diencephalon. Some of the nuclei of the hypothalamus are also found in the floor of the third ventricle. Input from all the sensory organs, except those associated with smell, synapse on (connect to) nuclei in the thalamus, which then relay information to the cerebral cortex. Some of the functions of the hypothalamus include control of the release of hormones from the **pituitary gland** and integration of the functions of the autonomic nervous system.

The Brainstem

Moving downward from the base of the diencephalon, the three divisions of the **brainstem** are the **midbrain**, pons, and medulla oblongata. Throughout the length of the brainstem, a weblike network of neurons called the **reticular formation** lies beneath the floor of the fourth ventricle. Within the reticular formation are several areas that relate to cardiovascular and respiratory control, sleep, consciousness, and alertness. Because these are such critical functions, damage to the brainstem can be lethal.

Areas of the midbrain play a role in eye movement, perception of pain, regulation of body temperature, and organization of simple movements. Along with the pons, the midbrain also helps control the sleep/wake cycle. Within the pons are areas that initiate dreaming and sleep, regulate attention level, and integrate the sensory and motor functions of the ear, eye, tongue, and facial muscles. The medulla controls limb position and head orientation, regulates breathing and heart rate, and integrates certain reflexes, such as sneezing, swallowing, and coughing.

Ten of the nuclei of the **cranial nerves** (*cranial* refers to the skull), which perform sensory and motor functions for the head and neck, are found in the brainstem (Table 3.3). All of the cranial nerves are considered to be part of the peripheral nervous system. However, the olfactory bulb and tract and the optic nerve are considered to be part of the central nervous system as well.

The Cerebellum

Sitting below the occipital lobe and atop the fourth ventricle is the cerebellum, a structure that looks much like a smaller version of the cerebrum. Like the cerebral hemispheres, the cerebellum is made up of a thin, folded cortex with underlying fiber tracts and groups of deep, paired nuclei. The cerebellum performs several critical functions, including coordination of movements, maintenance of posture, and the learning of motor skills. There is also evidence that the cerebellum may be involved in higher processes, such as thinking, reasoning, memory, speech, and emotions. High levels of alcohol (which is toxic) affect the cerebellum and cause a person to

TABLE 3.3 THE FUNCTIONS OF CRANIAL NERVES

CRANIAL NERVE	MAIN FUNCTIONS
I. Olfactory	Smell
II. Optic	Sight
III. Oculomotor	Eye movements and pupil and lens functions
IV. Trochlear	Eye movements
V. Trigeminal	Facial sensation and chewing
VI. Abducens	Eye movements
VII. Facial	Taste and facial expression
VIII. Vestibulocochlear	Hearing and equilibrium
IX. Glossopharyngeal	Taste and swallowing
X. Vagus	Speech, swallowing, and visceral sensory and motor functions
XI. Accessory	Head and shoulder movements
XII. Hypoglossal	Tongue movements

stagger and to display a wide stance to keep his or her balance. Because alcohol produces these typical effects, traffic officers often require people suspected of drinking and driving to try to walk a straight line, which is very difficult to do under the influence of alcohol.

THE CENTRAL NERVOUS SYSTEM: THE SPINAL CORD

The spinal cord makes up only about 2% of the volume of the central nervous system, but its functions are crucial. It relays sensory input to the brain and motor commands from the brain. Motor neurons in the spinal cord send commands to the muscles and internal organs. Referred to as **lower motor neurons**, these neurons are controlled by nerve signals from the upper motor neurons in the primary cortex. Other motor pathways that descend from the brain help to regulate the lower motor neurons. In a sense, the spinal cord is the link between the brain and the body.

The medulla transitions to the spinal cord at an opening in the base of the skull called the **foramen magnum**. The spinal cord takes up two-thirds of the length of the spinal canal and measures 42 to 45 cm (16.5 to 17.7 in) long, with a diameter of about 1 cm (0.4 in) at its widest point. It consists of 31 segments: 8 in the cervical region, 12 in the thoracic region, 5 in the lumbar region, 5 in the sacral region, and 1 in the coccygeal region.

Each segment of the spinal cord attaches to a pair of spinal nerves (Figure 3.3). Each spinal nerve has both a dorsal root made up of incoming sensory fibers and a ventral root made up of outgoing motor fibers. The dorsal root contains axons from a **dorsal root ganglion**, which is a cluster of neurons inside the spinal column close to where the dorsal root attaches to the spinal cord. Axons of sensory neurons in the body and the sense organs synapse on neurons in the dorsal root ganglion. Dorsal root ganglion neurons then send nerve signals to areas in the dorsal spinal cord that relay the sensory information to the brain. The ventral root contains the axons of motor

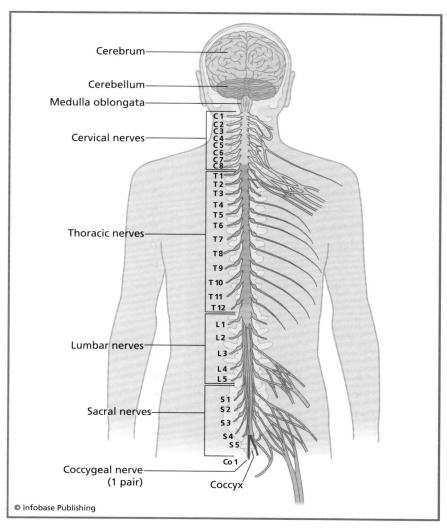

Cerebrum

Cerebellum

Medulla oblongata

Cervical nerves

C 1
C 2
C 3
C 4
C 5
C 6
C 7
C 8

T 1
T 2
T 3
T 4
T 5
T 6
Thoracic nerves
T 7
T 8
T 9
T 10
T 11
T 12

L 1
L 2
Lumbar nerves
L 3
L 4
L 5

S 1
Sacral nerves
S 2
S 3
S 4
S 5

Co 1

Coccygeal nerve
(1 pair)

Coccyx

© Infobase Publishing

Figure 3.3 The major divisions of the spinal cord are the cervical, thoracic, lumbar, sacral, and coccygeal regions.

neurons located in the ventral spinal cord. The two roots of each spinal nerve fuse before they exit the spinal canal through the particular intervertebral foramen that is associated with the spinal cord segment to which it is attached.

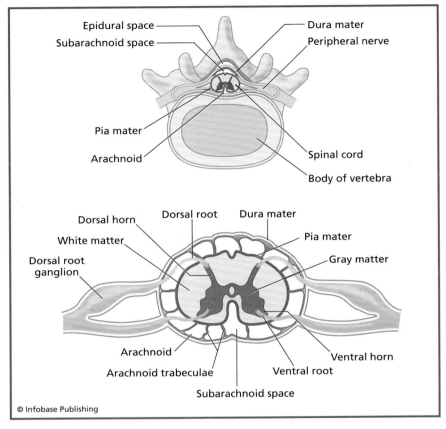

Figure 3.4   This cross section of the spinal cord shows the butterfly-shaped gray matter surrounded by white matter. Fiber tracts traveling to and from the brain are found in the white matter. Also shown are the meningeal membranes (pia mater, arachnoid, and dura mater) that surround the spinal cord and are continuous with those surrounding the brain. The axons of the dorsal root ganglion neurons carry sensory information to the dorsal spinal cord through the dorsal root of the spinal nerve. Axons of the motor neurons in the ventral spinal cord leave through the ventral root. The fusion of these two roots forms the spinal nerve, which emerges from the vertebral column through an intervertebral foramen.

A cross section of the spinal cord shows a butterfly-shaped area of gray matter around the small central spinal canal (Figure 3.4). Neurons that receive pain and sensory input are found in the dorsal "wings" of the butterfly; motor neurons that produce muscle movement are located in the ventral "wings." Surrounding the gray matter is the spinal cord's white matter, which consists of fiber tracts that run to and from the brain as well as fibers that travel locally within a particular section of the spinal cord.

As in the brain, three protective layers of membranes called meninges cover the spinal cord. Tough and inflexible, the **dura mater** lines the skull and the vertebral canal. Lining the dura mater is the **arachnoid membrane**, which sends thin, spidery extensions of connective tissue called **arachnoid trabeculae** to the delicate **pia mater**, the layer that adheres to the surface of the spinal cord and the brain. Extensions from the pia mater anchor the spinal cord to the dura mater. Between the pia mater and the arachnoid layer is the **subarachnoid space**. There, the cerebrospinal fluid flows around the brain and spinal cord.

WHAT IS LATERALIZATION OF FUNCTION?

Lateralization of function, or **hemispheric dominance**, refers to the dominant role of one or the other cerebral hemisphere in a particular function. For some functions, such as fine motor control and sensory input, neither hemisphere is dominant—the hemisphere opposite to the body structure is in charge. For example, the right hemisphere sends the commands that control the movement of the left fingers and receives sensory information from the left side of the body. However, one hemisphere may be more important in controlling certain functions than the other. That hemisphere is said to be dominant for a particular function. Language is a function for which the left hemisphere is dominant for over 95% of people. Other functions for which the left hemisphere is usually dominant are calculations and recognition of details in figures. Recognizing faces, expressing and experiencing emotions, and visual-spatial abilities are functions for which the right hemisphere is dominant.

THE PERIPHERAL NERVOUS SYSTEM

Along with the optic and olfactory nerves and the 10 pairs of cranial nerves that exit the brainstem, the nerves (and their nerve roots) that exit the spinal cord are considered part of the peripheral nervous system. Sensory neurons and their axons, as well as the axons of motor neurons in the spinal cord and preganglionic neurons located in the central nervous system, are all part of the peripheral nervous system. The peripheral nervous system has two divisions: the **somatic nervous system** and the **autonomic nervous system**.

The somatic nervous system includes sensory neurons and sensory and motor nerves of voluntary muscles. The sensory nerves transmit information to the spinal cord from the sensory organs and from the sensory receptors in the skin, skeletal muscles, and joints. Axons of lower motor neurons that project from the spinal cord to voluntary muscles are also part of the somatic nervous system and control voluntary muscle movements.

The autonomic nervous system has three divisions: the **sympathetic nervous system (SNS)**, the **parasympathetic nervous system (PNS)**, and the **enteric nervous system (ENS)**. The sympathetic nervous system makes energy available to the body during periods of stress or emotional events. It produces the physiological changes that prepare the body for what is called the "fight or flight" response, in which the body gears up to either face or run away from danger. These changes include sweating, an increase in heart rate and blood pressure, a widening (dilation) of the pupils for better vision at a distance, a shifting of blood flow to the brain and muscles, and the activation of the adrenal medulla, which is considered a sympathetic ganglion because it develops from the neural crest.

The actions of the parasympathetic nervous system are the opposite of those of the sympathic division: It conserves energy and helps the body return to normal after a stressful event. The parasympathetic nervous system serves a maintenance function. It is always working. The effects it produces on the body include an increase of blood flow to the intestines, slowing of the heart rate, and constriction of the pupils for closer vision. It brings the body functions back to normal after the sympathetic nervous system has been activated.

Motor commands to the smooth, or involuntary, muscle of the body organs and the glands originate in autonomic neurons in the spinal cord gray matter and in the motor nuclei of three cranial nerves (facial, oculomotor, and vagus). Like the motor neurons in the spinal cord, they are influenced by axons of neurons in the brain. Autonomic neurons in the spinal cord are known as *preganglionic neurons*. Their axons exit the spinal cord through the ventral root and connect to *postganglionic neurons* in the peripheral nervous system that relay the nerve signal to the target organ.

Preganglionic neurons of the sympathetic nervous system (*thoracolumbar system*) are located in the thoracic and lumbar spinal cord segments in the intermediolateral gray matter, which is located between the dorsal and ventral horns, or "butterfly wings." Most of the ganglia to which they project are located in a chain that lies parallel to and close to the spinal column. These ganglia then send long axons to the target organs. An exception is the adrenal medulla, which is considered a sympathetic ganglion because of its origin in the neural crest. Its neurons secrete hormones that augment the sympathetic response.

Preganglionic neurons of the parasympathetic nervous system (*craniosacral system*) are found in the facial, oculomotor, and vagus nerves and in the intermediolateral gray matter of sacral spinal cord segments. The ganglia to which the preganglionic parasympathetic neurons in the vagus nerve nuclei and in the sacral spinal cord project are located close to the target organs. Parasympathetic preganglionic neurons in the facial nerve nuclei are involved in salivation and those in the oculomotor nerve nuclei in dilation of the pupil. Branches of the vagus nerve innervate (stimulate) postganglionic neurons in or adjacent to glands of the head and neck, as well as most of the organs found in the chest and abdomen.

The ENS consists of neuronal networks within the walls and underneath the lining of the gastrointestinal tract. These networks operate independently of the central nervous system. The brain and the ENS communicate back and forth with each other via the vagus nerve, but the ENS can perform its functions even if the vagus nerve is cut. The ENS has its own sensory neurons, motor neurons, and interneurons, and it uses a variety of neurotransmitters. It even sends nerves to the pancreas and gallbladder to help regulate their activities. The messages sent by the ENS to the brain through the vagus nerve appear to have an effect on brain functions as well.

NEUROTRANSMITTERS

As noted previously, the neural signal has two components: an electrical signal that travels down the axon, and a chemical signal that crosses the synapse. For a neurochemical to be classified as a neurotransmitter, it has to meet certain criteria. It must be synthesized by the transmitting, or presynaptic, neuron, and it must be stored inside presynaptic vesicles in the presynaptic terminal. A neurotransmitter must be released from the presynaptic terminal by mechanisms that require calcium ions to be present. These calcium ions enter the presynaptic terminal when the arrival of an action potential depolarizes it. The neurochemical must selectively activate specific receptors, causing a change in the membrane potential of the postsynaptic membrane. Finally, there have to be mechanisms that remove the neurotransmitter from the synapse after release, either by reuptake (via specific transporters) into the presynaptic terminal or by being broken down by specific enzymes in the postsynaptic membrane. Dozens of neurochemicals meet all of these criteria.

Most neurotransmitters fall into one of four basic groups, depending on their chemical structure: **acetylcholine**, **monoamines**, amino acids, and peptides. Because its more complex structure contains an amine group, acetylcholine is sometimes placed with the monoamines into an "amine" group. Table 3.4 contains a list of neurotransmitters in the different groups. Neurotransmitters function by producing depolarizing postsynaptic membrane potentials (excitatory) or hyperpolarizing postsynaptic potentials (inhibitory). The same neurotransmitter can have an excitatory effect when it binds to one type of receptor and an inhibitory effect when it binds to another type. Whether the effect is excitatory or inhibitory depends on which ion channels are opened when the neurotransmitter binds to the cell's receptors. If sodium ions enter the cell, the postsynaptic membrane becomes depolarized. Chloride ions and potassium ions, in contrast, have a hyperpolarizing effect on the postsynaptic membrane and, hence, an inhibitory effect on the neuron's activity.

Acetylcholine

Acetylcholine was the first neurotransmitter to be discovered. The presynaptic terminals of all motor neurons release acetylcholine, and so do those of all autonomic preganglionic neurons, all parasympathetic postganglionic neurons, and the sympathetic postganglionic neurons that innervate the sweat glands. A number of nuclei in the brain produce and release acetylcholine. Acetylcholine is produced when an acetate molecule is attached to a choline molecule by a reaction involving the enzyme choline acetyltransferase. In the synapse, acetylcholine is broken down by acetylcholinesterase.

In general, cholinergic fibers (fibers that release acetylcholine) have an activating or facilitating effect on the functions of other brain structures. Cholinergic transmission increases the arousal of the cerebral cortex and is therefore important in the attentional component of learning and memory. Initiation

TABLE 3.4 TRANSMITTERS IN THE HUMAN BRAIN

Amines

Acetylcholine
Dopamine
Epinephrine
Histamine
Norepinephrine
Serotonin

Amino Acids

Aspartate
Gamma-aminobutyric acid (GABA)
Glycine
L-glutamate

Neuropeptides

Adrenocorticotropic hormone
  (ACTH)
Adrenomedullin
Amylin
Angiotensin II
Apelin
Bradykinin
Calcitonin
Calcitonin gene-related peptide
  (CGRP)
Cholecystokinin (CCK)
Corticotropin-releasing factor
  (CRF) (urocortin)
Dynorphins, neoendorphins
Endorphins, (lipotropic hormones
  [LPHs])
Endothelins
Enkephalins
Follicle-stimulating hormone
  (FSH)
Galanin
Gastric inhibitory peptide (GIP)
Gastrin
Gastrin-releasing peptide
Glucagonlike peptides (GLPs)
Gonadotropin-releasing hormone
  (GnRH)

Growth hormone-releasing factor
  (GHRF)
Lipotropin hormone (LPH)
Luteinizing hormone (LH)
Melanin-concentrating hormone
  (MCH)
Melanin-stimulating hormone
  (MSH)
Motilin
Neurokinins
Neuromedins
Neurotensin (NT)
Neuropeptide FF (NPFF)
Neuropeptide Y (NPY)
Orexins/hypocretins
Orphanin
Oxytocin
Nociceptin/FG
Pituitary adenylate cyclase-activat-
  ing polypeptide (PACAP)
Pancreatic polypeptide (PP)
Peptide histidine isoleucine (PHI)
Parathyroid hormone (PTH)
Peptide YY (PYY)
Prolactin releasing peptide (PrRP)
Secretin/PHI
Somatostatin (SS) (cortistatin)
Tachykinins
Thyroid-stimulating hormone
  (TSH)
Thyroid-releasing hormone (TRH)
Urotensin II
Vasopressin
Vasoactive intestinal peptide (VIP)

Others

Adenosine
Adenosine triphosphate
Anandamide
  (arachidonoylethanolamide)
Arachidonic acid
Nitric oxide

of rapid eye movements during one type of sleep is due to cholinergic projections from nuclei in the reticular formation. Cholinergic interneurons in the basal ganglia are important in movement.

Monoamines

The monoamines include **dopamine, norepinephrine**, epinephrine, and **serotonin**. Serotonin belongs to the indoleamine subclass, whereas the other three monoamines belong to the catecholamine subclass. The catecholamines are synthesized from the amino acid tyrosine in a series of enzymatic reactions that first produces L-DOPA, then dopamine, then norepinephrine, and finally epinephrine. **Monoamine oxidases** are enzymes that break down catecholamines. They are found in the blood and in catecholaminergic (activated by catecholamine) presynaptic terminals. All of the monoamines release their transmitters from varicosities, or beadlike swellings on their axons rather than at specific synapses.

Norepinephrine is produced and released by all postganglionic neurons of the sympathetic nervous system except those that innervate the sweat glands. Extensive projections from nuclei in the medulla, pons, and one thalamic region have an activating effect on other areas of the brain. They are also involved in appetite control and sexual behavior. The adrenal medulla makes and releases both norepinephrine and epinephrine into the bloodstream as hormones. These neurochemicals are an important part of the stress response, both as hormones and as neurotransmitters. Epinephrine is also synthesized by neurons in the medulla and in nuclei related to the vagus nerve. Some of the areas the vagus innervates, such as the hypothalamus and the preganglionic sympathetic neurons, have an important role in the stress response.

Dopamine may be either excitatory or inhibitory depending on which of its receptor subtypes is activated. It is produced by two structures in the midbrain: the substantia nigra

(SN) and the ventral tegmental area (VTA). Dopaminergic projections from the SN to the basal ganglia are important in movement. VTA neurons project to structures important in emotion, learning, and memory. The dopaminergic projections from the VTA to the nucleus accumbens is important in the brain's reward system. Some drugs, including cocaine, amphetamines, and methylphenidate, inhibit dopamine reuptake in the synapse and thereby increase the effects of dopamine.

Serotonin is involved in sleep, eating, arousal, dreaming, and the regulation of mood, body temperature, and pain transmission. It is made from the amino acid tryptophan by two enzymatic reactions. Nine clusters of serotinergic neurons are found in the raphe nuclei, which are located in the medulla, pons, and midbrain near the midline. Serotinergic neurons innervate the cerebral cortex, the basal ganglia, and the **dentate gyrus** of the hippocampus. Hallucinogenic drugs produce their effects by stimulating a receptor in the forebrain that is sensitive to serotonin.

Amino Acids

Glutamate, also known as glutamic acid, is the most abundant excitatory neurotransmitter in the central nervous system. It plays important roles in learning and memory, synaptic plasticity, and neurotoxicity. Glutamate is released at more than 90% of the brain's synapses and at the majority of spinal cord synapses. All sensory nerve endings release glutamate. It is synthesized from the amino acid tryptophan. Uptake of excess glutamate from the synapse is accomplished by specific transporters in the presynaptic membrane and in glial cell membranes. Inside glial cells, glutamate is converted into glutamine, which is then transported into glutamatergic terminals to be used for glutamate synthesis.

Gamma-amino butyric acid (GABA) is produced by the actions of enzymes on glutamic acid. It is released at over 90%

of the synapses in the brain that do not release glutamate. GABA is believed to have sedative, anxiety-relieving, muscle-relaxing, and anticonvulsant effects. It also causes amnesia, possibly because it inhibits the release of glutamate, which scientists believe is important in memory formation. It also inhibits the release of monoamines and acetylcholine, which facilitate the formation of memories by the brain. Glutamic acid decarboxylase (GAD) is the biosynthetic enzyme for GABA. Excess GABA is removed from the synapse by a specific transport system (primarily) or broken down enzymatically by specific enzymes inside postsynaptic neurons. GABA receptors are found on most CNS neurons, on astrocytes, and on autonomic nervous system neurons.

Glycine is the simplest amino acid. It is concentrated in the spinal cord, medulla, and retina. Unlike other neurotransmitters, glycine is found only in humans and other vertebrates. Neuroscientists currently know little about how glycine is synthesized. Reuptake transporters on glial cells remove glycine from the synaptic cleft. In addition to acting as an inhibitory neurotransmitter in the spinal cord and lower brain stem, glycine facilitates the activity of the NMDA (N-methyl D-aspartate) type of glutamatergic receptor. For the NMDA receptor to be activated, it is necessary that both glutamate and glycine bind to the receptor at their respective sites.

Both GABA and glycine help to maintain a balance in the nervous system. Although GABA is the main inhibitory transmitter in the brain, GABA and glycine are both important in the spinal cord. Left unchecked, glutamatergic excitatory transmission causes seizures and is neurotoxic (lethal to nerve cells). The lethal effects on cells of too much excitatory transmission and the free radicals that accompany it may be responsible for causing many diseases, such as cancer, inflammatory joint disease, diabetes, Parkinson's disease, and Alzheimer's disease. Free radicals have also been implicated in aging.

Neuropeptides

Neuropeptides are chains of linked amino acids that are produced in the brain. They are made from larger polypeptides that are cut into smaller segments by enzymes. There are three major groups of neuropeptides: endogenous opioids, peptides that are also found in the gastrointestinal tract (called gut peptides), and peptide hormones produced by the hypothalamus. Many peptides are found in presynaptic terminals with other neurotransmitters and may help modulate the effects of the other transmitters.

Endogenous opioids are produced by the brain. The term *opiates* is used for similar neuropeptides that are produced by plants or synthesized in the laboratory. The best known of the endogenous opioids are the *enkephalins*, which produce what is called the "runner's high"—the pleasurable feeling many athletes get from an intense workout. Other endogenous opioids are the *endorphins* and the *dynorphins*. When opioid receptors are activated, they cause analgesia (pain relief), euphoria (a feeling of extreme joy or elation), and also inhibit defensive responses such as hiding and fleeing. Synthetic opiates and opiates that come from plants act on the receptors that produce euphoria. Because they overstimulate the reward pathway in the brain, their use can lead to addiction. Although highly addictive, opiates such as morphine are sometimes used in the medical setting for their painkilling effects.

Drug Effects

Many drugs produce their effects by interacting with neurotransmitter receptors or related synaptic mechanisms. Some drugs, called **agonists**, actually mimic the effect of natural neurotransmitters by binding to the receptor and activating it. The results are very similar to those that the neurotransmitter itself would have produced. Other drugs, called **antagonists**, bind to the receptor without activating it. This prevents the neurotransmitter from binding to and activating the receptor.

Partial agonists bind to the receptor and produce a smaller effect than the neurotransmitter itself. **Inverse agonists** bind to the receptor and produce an effect opposite to the one that is usually associated with the receptor. **Indirect agonists** and antagonists increase or reduce, respectively, the level of neurotransmitter in the synapse. They do this by acting on reuptake transporters, on enzymes that break down excess neurotransmitter, or on synaptic vesicles in which neurotransmitter molecules are stored.

CONNECTIONS

Protected by bone and three layers of meninges, the brain and spinal cord make up the central nervous system. The central, lateral, and parieto-occipital sulci form the boundaries of the four lobes of the cerebral hemispheres: frontal, parietal, temporal, and occipital. Six layers of neurons make up the gray matter of the cerebral cortex, and their axons form most of the underlying white matter. Nuclei at the base of the cerebrum overlie the diencephalon, which in turn lies on top of the brainstem. Fiber tracts descend through the midbrain, pons, and medulla on their way to the spinal cord, the nuclei in the brainstem, and the cerebellum, which overlies the fourth ventricle. The peripheral nervous system is made up of all the components of the nervous system located outside the brain and spinal cord, including the 12 pairs of cranial nerves and the 31 pairs of spinal nerves. The peripheral nervous system has two divisions: somatic and autonomic. Sensory neurons and motor nerves that activate the skeletal muscles make up the somatic nervous system. Nerves of the autonomic nervous system regulate the viscera (internal organs) and the glands. The enteric nervous system regulates the movements of the gastrointestinal tract. Neurotransmitters are the nervous system's chemical messengers. When they are released from the presynaptic terminals of neurons into the synaptic cleft, they bind to and activate postsynaptic receptors that are specific to

(continues)

(continued)

each neurotransmitter. Glutamate is the most abundant excitatory neurotransmitter in the nervous system, and GABA is the major inhibitory neurotransmitter. Glycine is an important inhibitory neurotransmitter in the spinal cord. Acetylcholine, norepinephrine, dopamine, and serotonin increase the activation of parts of the cerebral cortex and also play roles in the sleep/wake cycle. Norepinephrine and epinephrine are important in the stress response, both as neurotransmitters and as hormones.

4

Sensation and Perception

IN THE AUTUMN, WE ARE AWED BY THE DAZZLING ARRAY OF leaf colors. In the winter, the intricate patterns of snowflakes and the beauty of the snow amaze us. Spring and summer flowers with their colors and aromas and the butterflies they attract bring us pleasure. We listen to the birds singing in the trees and the sounds the wind makes as it rustles the leaves and grass. The ocean waves and their roar fill us with wonder as we walk along the beach and feel the sand beneath our feet. When we wade into the water, the tide tugs at our ankles as we enjoy the cool ocean breeze on our faces.

All of these experiences are made possible by our senses, which take in information about our environment and send it to our brains to be integrated and interpreted. **Sensation** refers to the process by which stimuli are detected by the sense organs. The sense organs detect chemical and physical stimuli in the environment. These stimuli cause changes in the sensory receptors. **Transduction** is the process by which physical or chemical stimuli are translated into neural signals by the sensory receptors. **Perception** refers to the process in which the brain combines, organizes, and interprets sensations.

The ancient Greek philosopher Aristotle (384–322 B.C.) described five senses: vision, hearing, smell, taste, and touch. Modern scientists recognize several other senses, too, including equilibrium, pressure, temperature, position sense, and pain. Each of the senses has its own receptors, sensory neurons, and neural pathways, which transmit the stimuli to specific targets in the brain. Sensory information may be processed at two or more different levels once it reaches the brain. We are not consciously aware of these processing stages, only of the resulting perception.

VISION

Much like a camera, the eye focuses incoming light rays on a thin membrane at the back of the eye called the **retina**, which might be compared to the film in the camera (Figure 4.1). Most of the eyeball is covered by a tough white membrane called the **sclera**. Between the sclera and the retina is the **choroid**, a darkly pigmented layer filled with blood vessels, which provides nourishment to the retina. At the front of the eye, a transparent membrane called the **cornea** lets light into the eye. Its curvature helps focus the incoming light rays.

Behind the cornea is the pigmented **iris**, which gives the eyes their color. The circular muscles in this structure can contract to widen (dilate) or relax to narrow (constrict) the **pupil**—the opening at the center of the iris. Light passes through the pupil and through the transparent **lens**, which focuses the light

Figure 4.1 *(opposite page)* Our eyes are our "windows to the world." They are protected by the orbits, which are the bony sockets in the skull. The structures of the human eye are shown in the top diagram. The human eye can detect electromagnetic radiation in wavelengths between 380 and 760 nm (0.0001 to 0.00003 in.). This range of wavelengths is called the visible spectrum; it falls between ultraviolet rays and infrared rays on the electromagnetic spectrum *(bottom)*.

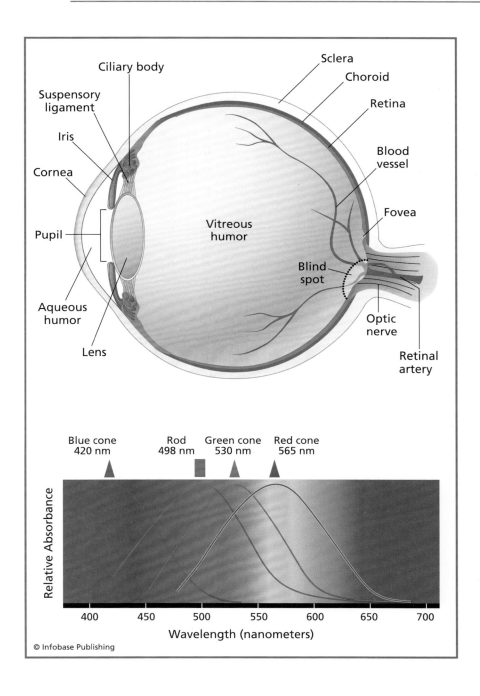

© Infobase Publishing

on the retina. Two muscles, one above and one below the lens, hold the lens in place and contract or relax to change the shape of the lens. The lens takes on a more spherical shape for near vision and a flatter shape for far vision.

The light reflected from an object is focused on the retina so that the image of the object is upside down and backward—much as it is on the film in a camera. The brain, however, reverses this image. In the space between the cornea and the lens, a fluid called the **aqueous humor** circulates to provide nutrition to the cornea and lens, which have no blood vessels of their own. It also maintains pressure inside the eye. Behind the lens, the space inside the eye is filled with the **vitreous humor**, a gel-like substance that maintains the shape of the eyeball.

At the rear of the retina is a single layer of receptor cells that contain **photopigments**. These pigments go through chemical changes when they are exposed to light. These chemical changes cause ion channels in the cell membrane to open so that the receptor cell depolarizes and fires an action potential. Two layers of essentially transparent neurons lie in front of the pigmented **photoreceptor** layer. The neural signal generated by each photoreceptor cell goes to a **bipolar cell** in the layer closest to the photoreceptor layer. Each bipolar cell then sends the signal on to a **ganglion cell** in the retinal layer closest to the vitreous humor. Axons from the ganglion cells of each eye converge to form the optic nerve. The point at which the optic nerve leaves the eyeball on its way to the brain is called the "blind spot" because there are no photoreceptor cells there.

Named for their shapes, the two types of photoreceptor cells in the eye are called **rods** and **cones**. The eye has approximately 125 million rods and 6 million cones. Rods contain a pigment called rhodopsin, which is sensitive to as little as one photon of light. (A photon is the smallest unit of light at a particular wavelength.) This extreme sensitivity allows us to see in dim light. Rods also help the eyes detect movement.

The eye has three types of cones, each of which has one of three different color pigments. Each color pigment is most sensitive to one of three colors: red, blue, or green. The relative activity of the three different kinds of cones is important in determining the color-coding signal that goes to the brain.

Visual acuity, or the ability to see details, is greatest in bright light when the cones are most active. It is poorest in dim light when the rods are most active. In dim light, the edges of objects appear blurred, and we see in tones of gray rather than colors.

Light rays that enter the eye focus on the center of the retina in an area called the **macula**. It is here that the cones are most heavily concentrated. In the center of the macula is a tiny circular area about 1 mm (0.04 in.) in diameter (the size of a pinhead). This site, called the **fovea**, is indented because cone receptors are the only cells present there. The fovea is located just above the point where the optic nerve leaves the eye. Outside the macula, the concentration of cones begins to decrease,

WHAT IS COLOR BLINDNESS?

Color blindness is the inability to distinguish between either red and green (most common) or yellow and blue. The absence of all color, when a person sees only in tones of gray, is very rare. The genes for the pigments of the red and green cones lie close together on the X chromosome, of which females have two copies and males have only one. Color blindness is a recessive trait, so a female would have to have defective genes on both X chromosomes for the trait to be expressed. Because this is unlikely, only about 0.4% of females are colorblind, whereas approximately 8% of males are colorblind.

The gene for the blue pigment is found on chromosome 7, which is present in duplicate in both sexes. As a result, this type of color blindness is less common, affecting about 1 person in 10,000. If the gene for one of the visual color pigments is defective or missing, that pigment will be expressed in reduced quantities in the cones of the retina or not expressed at all. As a result, the color-blind person will see the world in shades and combinations of the two color pigments that are expressed.

whereas the number of rods increases. The number of rods is greatest in an area that forms a circle at 20° from the fovea in all directions. Vision is sharpest in the fovea. Vision loses its sharpness as the density of cones decreases farther away from the fovea.

As the two optic nerves exit behind the eyes, they travel medially (toward the center) to the **optic chiasm**, just in front of the hypothalamus (Figure 4.2). There, the axons of the ganglion cells in the half of the retina closest to the nose (the nasal half) on each side cross and travel toward the opposite, or **contralateral**, side of the brain. The axons of the ganglion cells in the half of the retina closest to the temple (the temporal half) do not cross. Instead, they travel toward the same, or **ipsilateral**, side of the brain. As a result, visual information from the left side of the visual field of each eye ends up on the right side of the brain, and vice versa.

From the optic chiasm, 90% of the fibers on each side travel to the **lateral geniculate nucleus** of the thalamus on the ipsilateral side and synapse on neurons there. From this relay nucleus in the thalamus, the visual information is sent to the **primary visual cortex** where it is processed and then relayed to other areas of the brain to be further processed. All sensory inputs except olfactory (smell) go first to the thalamus before the signals travel to the cerebral cortex. The other 10% of the optic tract fibers reach other targets on the ipsilateral side, including targets involved in the control of eye movements and of body rhythms that are synchronized with the amount of light in the environment.

Axons from each lateral geniculate nucleus travel as an **optic radiation** through the temporal lobe back to the ipsilateral primary visual cortex, most of which is folded into the **calcarine fissure** at the pole of the occipital lobe. The **secondary visual cortex**, where processing of raw visual data begins, surrounds the primary visual cortex around the outside of the calcarine fissure. Projections from the visual cortex reach other areas of the cortex, allowing visual information to be integrated

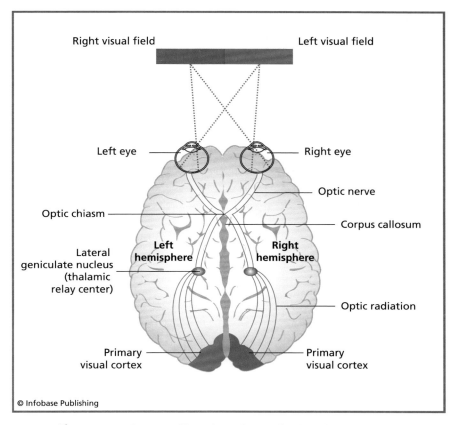

Figure 4.2   The nerve fibers from the nasal half of the retina of each eye cross to the other side of the brain in the optic chiasm. This results in visual information from each half of the visual field being represented in the opposite side of the brain.

with information from the other senses. It is estimated that in humans, 25 to 40% of the cerebral cortex plays some role in the processing of visual information.

Vision loss that results from damage to the central pathways varies with the specific location of the damage (lesion). If one optic nerve is completely cut, there will be blindness in the ipsilateral eye. Partial damage to the optic nerve causes a small blind spot called a scotoma. A person with this problem may not even notice it if it affects only the peripheral visual field. However, if it affects the fovea, there will be a noticeable reduction in the sharpness of vision. Damage to the optic chiasm, which often occurs as a result of pituitary tumors, causes a bilateral loss of the temporal half of the visual field. This affects peripheral vision. Again, the person affected may not realize there is a problem unless he or she has an accident because of the peripheral vision loss. A lesion of the primary visual cortex, which is usually caused by stroke or a blow to the back of the head, causes vision loss in the contralateral half of the visual field, usually with macula sparing.

HEARING

The many sounds in our environment range from the quiet tick of a clock to the roar of a jet engine or a clap of thunder. Sound waves travel through the air at about 767 miles (1,235 kilometers) per hour (Figure 4.3). They are funneled into the ear canal by the **pinna**—the external structure composed of skin and cartilage that we normally refer to as the ear. At the end of the ear canal is a thin membrane called the **tympanic membrane**, or **eardrum**. All of these structures together make up what is known as the **outer ear**. When sound waves reach the eardrum, they make it vibrate. These vibrations are transmitted across the air-filled space of the **middle ear** by means of a series of three tiny bones, the **ossicles**. These bones are named for their shapes: the *malleus* (hammer), *incus* (anvil), and *stapes* (stirrup). The malleus is attached to the eardrum, and the stapes is attached to the membrane that covers the inside of the *oval window*. The oval window opens into the fluid-filled **cochlea**, or inner ear. Opposite the cochlea is a set of bony canals that are involved in the sense of balance.

Sound waves produced by the vibration of objects in the environment are detected by the human ear in the range of 30 to 20,000 vibrations per second. Unlike the eye, which combines wavelengths to produce the perception of a single color, the ear does not combine the frequencies it receives, but hears

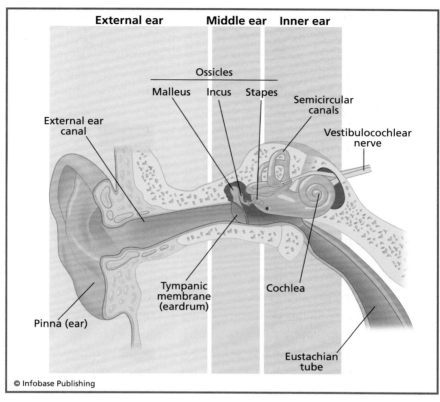

Figure 4.3   The human ear includes the outer (or external), middle, and inner ear sections. Sound waves produced by the vibrations of objects in the environment enter the outer ear and strike the eardrum, which separates the outer ear from the middle ear. The sound waves cause the eardrum to vibrate, and the vibrations are transmitted to the inner ear via the ossicles. In the cochlea of the inner ear, these vibrations are transduced to (changed into) electrical impulses, which are sent to the brain, where they are interpreted as sound.

them as separate tones. Because most of us cannot move our ears, we turn our heads to hear better, an action that allows the outer ear to be a more efficient "sound funnel." Tiny muscles attached to the stapes and malleus react reflexively to loud noises by contracting, causing the chain of ossicles to stiffen and the eardrum to become more taut. This results in less low-frequency sound being transmitted by the ossicles and more being reflected by the eardrum. It is thought that this helps protect the ear from damage. Some scientists think that the reflex selectively filters low-frequency transmission to reduce background "noise," thus enabling a person to hear meaningful sounds better.

The cochlea is a bony structure that resembles a snail shell in shape. It contains the receptor cells and auditory neurons that collect sound wave data and convert it into neural signals. If the "coil" of the cochlea were straightened out, we would see two membranes extending the length of the coil. The lower, flexible membrane is called the *basilar membrane*. Embedded in this basilar membrane are hair cells. These are the receptors for the auditory, or hearing, sense. Suspended above the basilar membrane is the rigid *tectorial membrane*. Together, the basilar membrane, tectorial membrane, and hair cells make up what is called the **organ of Corti**.

As the oval window vibrates in response to the movement of the stapes against it, the fluid that fills the cochlea and circulates around the basilar membrane moves. This, in turn, causes the basilar membrane to vibrate. Hairlike structures called cilia at the tip of each hair cell are embedded in the tectorial membrane above them. As the basilar membrane moves beneath the hair cells, these cilia bend. This causes potassium ion channels in the hair cell to open and generate an action potential.

Because they have no axons, auditory hair cells synapse directly on the dendrites of bipolar neurons whose axons form the cochlear nerve, which merges with the auditory nerve. Neurotransmitter molecules released from the bases of the hair cells transmit the signal by binding to receptors on the auditory neurons. The pathway of the auditory neural signal to the brain is complex. It branches several times to synapse on structures along the way. As a result, each structure in this complicated pathway receives auditory information from both ears. One of these structures is the **medial geniculate nucleus**, which is located in the thalamus. From the medial geniculate nuclei, the auditory information is transmitted to the primary auditory cortex, which is found in the posterior superior temporal lobe at the edge of and extending into the lateral fissure. Projections from the primary auditory cortex go to the surrounding secondary auditory cortex. The higher-order auditory cortex surrounds the secondary auditory cortex and extends laterally to the edge of the superior temporal sulcus. Processing of auditory information is hierarchical, in that the processing of sounds, ranging from simple tones to speech perception, becomes increasingly complex at each ascending level. Projections from the auditory association cortex to the polymodal cortex, which lies inside the superior temporal sulcus, allow the integration of auditory information with visual information and information from the body senses. As with visual information, auditory information reaches multiple areas of the cortex for integration with other sensory information.

In the left temporal lobe, there is an area of the higher-order auditory cortex known as **Wernicke's area**, or *speech receptive area*. If this area is damaged, the person experiences a loss of speech *comprehension*. The equivalent area in the right temporal lobe interprets emotional aspects of language. Other higher-order auditory areas extend from the temporal lobe up into the lower parietal lobe. They are important in writing and reading. Projections from auditory primary and secondary areas go to **Broca's area**, or the motor speech area, located on the other side of the lateral fissure in the lower frontal lobe on the left side of the brain. Damage to this area results in an impairment of speech *production*—that is, speech becomes garbled or, with severe damage, completely absent.

Approximately 10% of adults suffer from some degree of deafness (loss of hearing). There are two basic types of deafness. *Conductive deafness* involves the middle ear or the outer ear canal. The most common causes are an overaccumulation of earwax (cerumen) or an inflammation in the middle ear. *Otosclerosis* is a less common form of conductive deafness. In this condition, the joint between the vestibule of the inner ear and the footplate of the stapes becomes rigid and bony (calcifies), making the stapes unable to move. *Sensorineural deafness* usually results when the neurons in the inner ear degenerate. This type of deafness can be caused by a noisy work environment, mumps or German measles infections, a tumor, or certain drugs (particularly antibiotics). Damage to auditory pathways does not usually produce deafness because of the bilateral projections from each ear to the brain structures involved in hearing.

EQUILIBRIUM

The sense of equilibrium, or balance, is called the *vestibular sense* because it is regulated by the vestibular system. The vestibular organs are part of the inner ear. Vestibular receptors are found in three semicircular canals opposite the cochlea, and also in two saclike structures called the utricle and saccule that are located in the **vestibule** adjacent to the cochlea. The cilia of the vestibular receptor cells are embedded in a gel-like mass called the *cupula*, which covers the hair cells. When the head turns, the movement of the fluid in the semicircular canals displaces the gelatinous mass, making the cilia bend. In the saccule and utricle, calcium carbonate crystals within the gelatinous mass lie on top of the cilia. When the head moves forward, these crystals move and bend the cilia, which send signals to the bipolar neurons of the vestibular ganglion, which relay the information about the change in the head's position to the vestibular nuclei in the medulla and the pons.

Sensory pathways from the vestibular nuclei help control neck and head position by sending the brain information about body and visual orientation. Vestibular sensory information goes first to the ventral posterior nuclei of the thalamus on both sides of the brain and from there to the parietal lobe and the **insula**. Two motor pathways descend from the vestibular nuclei to the spinal cord. One of these pathways, the *lateral vestibulospinal tract*, reaches neurons in the spinal cord at all levels. It is crucial in the control of balance and posture. The other pathway, called the *medial vestibulospinal tract*, travels to the cervical and upper thoracic areas of the spinal cord and helps control head position. Other fibers from the vestibular nuclei go to the cerebellum, the reticular formation, the motor nuclei that control the eye muscles, and back to the vestibular organ itself. *Motion sickness* involves the projection to the reticular formation. Projections to the oculomotor nuclei cause reflex adjustments of eye movements as the head moves. If the vestibular system malfunctions, we can experience vertigo (dizziness) and problems with balance.

TASTE

Taste, or *gustation*, and smell are known as the chemical senses because their receptors respond to chemical stimuli. All of the other senses respond to physical stimuli. The sense of taste serves two important functions: to meet our nutritional needs by detecting food molecules dissolved in saliva and to detect poisons in ingested substances. There are four basic taste qualities: sweet, salty, sour, and bitter. There is also a fifth taste quality called *umami* (Japanese for "delicious") that has recently been identified. Umami is the taste quality associated with the amino acid glutamate and salts of glutamate, such as monosodium glutamate, or MSG. (Some foods, such as fish, tomatoes, cheese, corn, peas, and human milk, contain glutamate naturally.) A particular flavor is a combination of one or more of the five basic taste qualities. Taste and smell both contribute to our perception of flavor. In fact, smell plays the greater role. You can find this out for yourself. Try holding your nose while tasting some familiar foods. How do they taste now?

Altogether, there are about 10,000 **taste buds** on the surface of the tongue, roof of the mouth, pharynx, epiglottis, larynx, and upper esophagus. Most of these taste buds are associated with the taste papillae (singular: *papilla*) that appear as tiny red bumps on the surface of the tongue (Figure 4.4). All taste buds can detect all five taste qualities. Some, however, are more sensitive to one taste quality than to the others. Hence, a simplistic "taste map" of the tongue shows the tip of the tongue as more sensitive to sweet and salty tastes, the sides of the tongue to

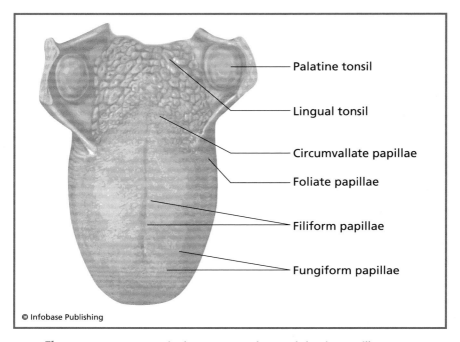

- Palatine tonsil
- Lingual tonsil
- Circumvallate papillae
- Foliate papillae
- Filiform papillae
- Fungiform papillae

© Infobase Publishing

Figure 4.4   Most taste buds are arranged around the tiny papillae or "bumps" on the surface of the tongue. They are found in the moatlike trenches of the circumvallate papillae, inside the folds of the foliate papillae, and on the surface of the mushroom-shaped fungiform papillae. Conelike filiform papillae are the most numerous but do not contain taste buds. Although fewer in number than the other papillae, the circumvallate papillae contain almost half of the approximately 5,000 taste buds on the tongue.

sour tastes, and the back of the tongue and back of the mouth to bitter tastes.

Each taste bud is an onion-shaped cluster of about 100 taste receptor cells. These structures do the actual work of detecting taste sensations. Each of these cells lives for about 1 to 2 weeks before dying and being replaced. From 3 to 250 taste buds can be found on the sides or top of each taste papilla. Taste buds found in the anterior third of the tongue are innervated by the *chorda tympani* branch of the facial nerve, those from the posterior third of the tongue by the glossopharyngeal nerve, and those found in the larynx and epiglottis by the vagus nerve.

Fibers carrying taste information travel to the solitary nucleus in the medulla, where they synapse on neurons that send taste information to the ipsilateral ventral posterior medial nucleus of the thalamus. (Some fibers that leave the solitary nucleus travel to the motor nuclei of cranial nerves. These participate in coughing, swallowing, and other reflexes related to taste.) Taste information is then relayed from the thalamus to the **insular cortex** and frontal lobe operculum. Information from the gustatory cortex goes to the orbital cortex in the frontal lobe for integration with olfactory information and to the amygdala, from which the information is relayed to the hypothalamus and other areas associated with emotion and memory.

Individuals differ in the number of taste buds they have by 100-fold. As we get older, the number of taste receptors we have gradually declines. The sense of taste can be impaired by smoking, gingivitis, strep throat, influenza, deficiencies of vitamin B_{12} or zinc, side effects of certain drugs, or injuries to the head or mouth. A partial loss of the sense of taste is called **hypogeusia**. The total loss of all taste sensation is called **ageusia**.

SMELL

The sense of smell, or *olfaction*, is activated by airborne molecules that are detected by **olfactory receptors**—proteins that span the membranes of the cilia of **primary olfactory neurons** in the lining of the nasal cavity. There are about 3 million of these neurons in each nostril, residing in two patches that are each a few centimeters square and located directly below the eyes. Primary olfactory neurons live for about a month before they are replaced by neurons that develop from stem cells known as *basal cells*. There are about 350 types of olfactory receptors, which together can detect up to 10,000 different odors. However, only one type of receptor appears on any given olfactory neuron. Each type of olfactory receptor appears to respond to multiple *odorants*, or gaseous chemicals.

Primary olfactory neuronal axons travel up through tiny openings in the **cribriform plate** to synapse in clusters on the paired olfactory bulbs on the underside of the frontal lobe. Axons from the olfactory bulb neurons travel through the **olfactory tract** to the ipsilateral primary olfactory cortex, which includes the olfactory nucleus, the amygdala, and areas in the temporal lobe and ventral frontal cortex. Some of these structures play a role in emotion regulation and in memory. Unlike sensory information from the other sense organs, smell signals travel first to the primary olfactory cortex before going to the thalamus. However, olfactory messages go to the dorsomedial nucleus of the thalamus on their way from the primary olfactory cortex to the secondary olfactory cortex, which is located in the orbital cortex and adjacent insula, near the gustatory cortex (Figure 4.5).

Viruses, some medications, head injuries, and chemicals such as insecticides, chlorine, benzene, and mercury can destroy primary olfactory neurons in the nasal cavity. We also gradually lose some of our sense of smell as we age. Early symptoms of Parkinson's disease and Alzheimer's disease include an impaired sense of smell. A complete loss of the sense of smell is called **anosmia**, whereas a partial loss is called **hyposmia**.

BODY SENSES

The body senses, or somatosenses, include touch, pressure, vibration, pain, sense of position, and awareness of movement. The cell bodies of the neurons that receive information from the body senses are found in the sense organs and in ganglia in the brainstem and near the spinal cord. Their axons leave the brainstem as the sensory component of certain cranial nerves, and they leave the spinal cord as the sensory component of spinal nerves. Cranial nerves that supply the skin, muscles, and other tissues of the head and neck have sensory fibers that carry information from somatosensory receptors to the brain as well as from motor fibers to muscles. Each dorsal root ganglion neuron has an axonal process that enters the spinal cord and synapses on spinal cord neurons and has a long dendritic process that reaches to the peripheral organs and tissues.

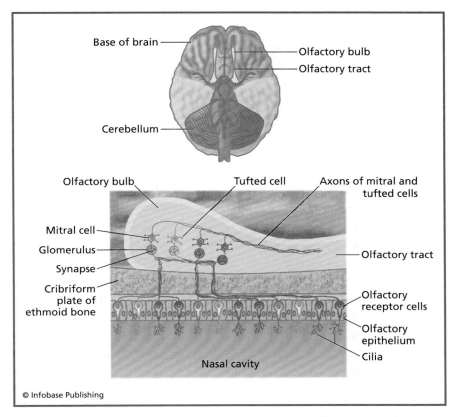

Figure 4.5 The axons of olfactory neurons travel in small bundles up through tiny openings in the cribriform ("perforated") plate of the ethmoid bone to synapse on neurons in the olfactory bulb. The axons from cells in the olfactory bulb travel through the olfactory tract to the primary olfactory cortex.

After many branchings, the fine endings of these dendritic processes act as sensory receptors for the skin, visceral organs, and other body tissues.

Surrounding each peripheral nerve is a three-layered sheath of connective tissue that is continuous with the meninges of the brain and spinal cord. Around some somatosensory nerve endings is a capsule (sheath). Depending on the type of receptor, the capsule is part of either the outer layer (which is continuous with the dura mater) or the middle layer (which is continuous with the arachnoid membrane). These nerve endings are said to be encapsulated somatosensory receptors. Some nerve ending capsules are thin. Others are layered—some elaborately so. All nerve endings are covered with the nerve sheath's inner layer, which is continuous with the pia mater. Nerve endings that have no capsule are called **free nerve endings**, or unencapsulated somatosensory receptors.

Free nerve endings are found in the skin, in the pulp around the teeth, in the muscles and internal organs, and in the membranes that cover the muscles, bones, joints, and organs and line the body cavity. Depending on where they are located, these tiny branching dendritic ends can transduce mechanical (touch, pressure, vibration, and stretch), thermal (temperature), chemical (prostaglandins), and pain stimuli into neural signals.

Free nerve endings in the skin wrap around the bases of individual hairs and are activated when the hairs bend. Pain is also detected by free nerve endings in the skin and elsewhere. **Merkel's disks,** with disk-shaped endings, are found in the basal layer of the epidermis (the outer layer of the skin). Abundant in the lips and fingertips, they are sensitive to light pressure and are important in detecting rough textures, shapes, and edges of objects that are not moving. **Meissner's corpuscles,** with elongated capsules, are found just below the epidermis. They are found in the fingers, palms of the hands, and soles of the feet. Particularly abundant in the fingertips, their sensitivity to low-frequency vibrations allows them to detect the texture of objects as the skin moves over them (and vice versa). **Pacinian corpuscles** are found just beneath the skin and in other connective tissues, including muscles and joints. In cross section, they look like a cut onion. With as many as 70 layers wrapped around the dendritic ending, they are the largest sensory receptors in the body. Their sensitivity to high-frequency vibration allows them to detect fine textures and other stimuli as they move across the skin. **Ruffini's corpuscles**, which sense stretch, have cigar-shaped capsules. Found in the dermis (the skin layer beneath the epidermis) and in tendons and ligaments, Ruffini's corpuscles are sensitive to the stretching of the skin and ligaments during movement of the fingers, toes, or limbs.

In addition to having many free nerve endings, muscle tissue has two specialized encapsulated receptors: the **muscle spindles** and the **Golgi tendon organs**. Muscle spindles are scattered throughout all of the skeletal muscles. These thin, long stretch receptors are made up of a few muscle fibers with a capsule around the middle third of the structure. Muscle fibers involved in skeletal movement are called **extrafusal muscle fibers**. Attached at their ends to the extrafusal muscle fibers, the fibers of the muscle spindles are called **intrafusal muscle fibers**. When an extrafusal muscle is extended, the muscle spindles are stretched. This causes ion channels to open and generate a neural signal.

The muscle spindles detect changes in muscle length, whereas Golgi tendon organs detect muscle tension. Found at the point where tendons and muscles meet, these spindle-shaped receptors are similar in structure to Ruffini's corpuscles. Surprisingly, research has shown that it is the muscle spindles—not the Golgi tendon organs—that are more important in **proprioreception**, our sense of body position, and in **kinesthesia**, the sense that makes us aware of our body movements.

Pain receptors, or **nociceptors**, detect intense or painful stimuli. These stimuli may be mechanical (cutting or pinching), thermal (cold or hot), or chemicals *(prostaglandins)* that the body releases into damaged tissue. Individual nociceptors may detect only one of these types of stimuli, or they may detect all three. Nociceptors are present in the skin, the membranes around bones, muscle sheaths, artery walls, the dura mater, and the membranes that cover and line internal organs and body cavities.

Nociceptors are the free nerve endings of pain fibers. These nerve endings can be further sensitized by chemicals released into the tissues after injury. This may explain why injured areas, such as sunburned skin, are sensitive to touch. There are no pain receptors in the brain itself or in the actual tissues of the internal organs. Thus, patients are often kept awake during brain surgery because they feel no pain from the procedure.

Two types of fibers associated with two different types of pain branch into the free nerve endings that are nociceptors. A-delta fibers, which are small in diameter and thinly myelinated, are responsible for "fast pain"—the sharp, stabbing pain that immediately alerts the body that an injury has occurred. C fibers, which are very small and unmyelinated, send their signals more slowly. They are responsible for slow, recurring, or aching pain.

Signals from both types of pain fibers travel first to the dorsal root ganglion neurons, the axons of which synapse on nociceptor neurons in the dorsal horns of the spinal cord gray matter. Axons from the nociceptor neurons in the spinal cord cross to the contralateral side and then travel up the spinal cord to the brainstem.

Pain information from A-delta fibers travels directly to the ventral posteriolateral nucleus of the thalamus and from there to the somatosensory cortex. Pain information from C fibers takes a slow route through the reticular formation in the medulla and pons to the thalamus and hypothalamus and to other areas that connect with the amygdala and hypothalamus. Because areas such as the amygdala and hypothalamus are involved in emotion, some of these pathways may be involved in the emotions that are often associated with pain.

Touch and proprioceptive information from the head and face travel to the thalamus before ascending to the somatosensory cortex. The tract carrying pain information from the head and face travels to three thalamic nuclei, including the ventral posterior medial nucleus. It then ascends to the primary somatosensory cortex as well as to the insular cortex and the cingulate gyrus, both of which are thought to be involved in the emotional aspects of pain.

CONNECTIONS

Information transduced from internal and environmental stimuli by sensory receptors travels through dendritic fibers to the dorsal root ganglia and the sensory nuclei of the cranial nerves. Axons of dorsal root ganglion neurons synapse on neurons in the dorsal horns of the spinal cord. Dorsal horn neurons and cranial nerve sensory nuclei then project to the brain. Except for olfactory information, sensory signals go to the thalamus before being transmitted to the appropriate primary sensory cortices. Olfactory information goes to the primary olfactory cortex before it is relayed through the thalamus to the secondary olfactory cortex. The thalamic relay nuclei for the senses are the lateral geniculate nucleus for vision, the medial geniculate nucleus for hearing, the dorsomedial nucleus for olfaction (smell), the ventral posterior nucleus for the vestibular sense, the ventral posterior medial nucleus for taste and the somatosenses, and the ventral posteriolateral nucleus for pain.

The primary sensory cortex, where raw sensory data is interpreted, is found in the calcarine fissure for vision, inside the lateral sulcus for hearing, in the insula and parietal cortex for balance, in the insula and frontal operculum for taste, in the insula and cingulate cortex for pain, in the somatosensory cortex for the body senses other than pain, and in several anterior temporal areas for smell. The secondary sensory cortex is located around the outside of the calcarine fissure for vision; in the orbitofrontal cortex for taste and smell; in the lateral sulcus surrounding, and posterior to, its primary sensory area for hearing; and in the insular cortex and parietal operculum for the somatosenses. Higher-order centers process information of increasing complexity and integrate information from the different sensory modalities.

5

Movement

MANY OF THE INTERACTIONS WE HAVE WITH OUR PHYSICAL and social environments involve movement. During the developmental milestones of infancy, we develop the ability to make simple movements such as speaking, reaching, walking, or running. More complex movements—for example, typing, skiing, riding a bicycle, dancing, playing a musical instrument, or drawing—must be learned, but the individual steps you need to make the movements become automatic over time. Our nervous system controls all of these different kinds of movement through a complex set of interactions between the motor areas of the brain, the spinal cord, and the nerves and fiber pathways that connect them to each other and to the muscles.

MUSCLE TYPES

Our bodies have three basic types of muscles: skeletal, or striated, muscle; smooth muscle; and cardiac muscle.

Skeletal muscles are often described as **voluntary muscles** because we can consciously control most of our skeletal movements. The two ends of a skeletal muscle are usually attached to two different bones. When the muscle contracts, it moves the bone. Some movements of skeletal muscles, however, are involuntary responses to certain stimuli, particularly stimuli that signal danger. These responses are called **reflexes.** For example, when your hand jerks away from a hot stove, your muscles have responded reflexively to the danger—the heat that might burn your hand.

Smooth muscle and cardiac muscle are sometimes called **involuntary muscle** because they usually function automatically, without our conscious control. **Smooth muscle** is under the control of the autonomic nervous system, which is controlled by the hypothalamus. Smooth muscles in the eye control the size of the pupil and the shape of the lens. There are also smooth muscles around the hair follicles; in the sphincters of the urinary bladder and anus; and in the walls of the blood vessels and the digestive, urinary, and reproductive tracts.

Cardiac muscle is found only in the walls of the heart. Although it looks somewhat like striated muscle, it functions more like smooth muscle. The heartbeat is initiated independently of the nervous system by a cell group in the heart called the *pacemaker.* A denervated (deprived of a nerve supply) heart will continue to beat as long as blood flows through it. However, hormones and an autonomic nerve supply do modulate heart functions.

ANATOMY AND PHYSIOLOGY OF THE NEUROMUSCULAR SYSTEM

A muscle fiber is a bundle of **myofibrils**, which are made up of strands, or filaments, of myosin and actin molecules. These filaments interact to make muscles contract. The striations of skeletal muscles are the dark stripes formed where filaments of myosin and actin overlap. Each motor neuron sends an axon out through the ventral or motor root of the spinal cord or out from the brainstem (in the case of cranial nerves) to the muscle fibers that it synapses on and activates. The number of muscle fibers a particular motor neuron stimulates depends on how coarse or fine the movements involved are. The branched endings of a motor neuron may activate as many as

1,000 fibers in the large muscles of the thigh and hip, whereas another motor neuron may stimulate fewer than 10 fibers in the muscles of the fingers, where more precise movements are required. A **motor unit** consists of a motor neuron, its axon and nerve endings, and the set of muscle fibers that it activates (Figure 5.1).

A skeletal muscle is made up of a large group (up to several hundred) of parallel muscle fibers. The muscle is usually attached at its opposite ends to two different bones by bands of connective tissue called *tendons*. There is often a joint between the two bones. Some muscles make a limb bend, or flex; these kinds of muscles are called **flexors**. Other muscles cause a limb to straighten out, or extend; these are called **extensors**. For every flexor muscle there is an opposing extensor muscle. This rule also applies to muscles that attach to only one bone, such as the muscles of the eye and tongue. Sometimes groups of muscles attach across a joint and work as a group; these are known as **synergistic** muscles. In such cases, there is one group of synergistic flexor muscles and an opposing group of synergistic extensor muscles.

NERVOUS SYSTEM CONTROL OF MOVEMENT

Motor commands travel from the motor cortex down to the cranial nerve nuclei or the spinal cord and out to the muscle fibers. We will start in the brain and move downward as we look at the ways that the nervous system controls and coordinates muscle movements.

CEREBRAL CORTEX

Several areas of the cerebral cortex are important in movement control (Figure 5.2). The primary motor cortex is located in the precentral gyrus, which is in the frontal lobe just in front of the central sulcus. Studies of the brain have shown that every area of the body is represented here. Those parts of the body that perform finer movements, such as the lips and fingers, are much more heavily represented.

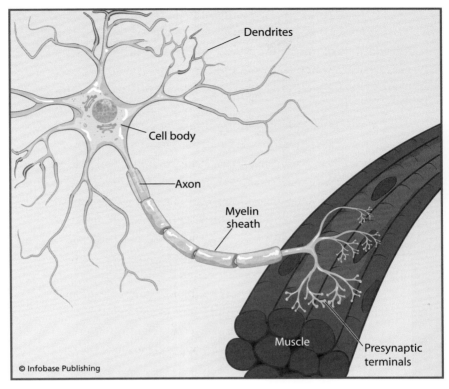

Dendrites

Cell body

Axon

Myelin
sheath

Muscle

Presynaptic
terminals

© Infobase Publishing

Figure 5.1   A single neuron can stimulate many fibers within a muscle. The number of fibers a neuron innervates depends on how fine the motor control of a particular muscle is. The finer the motor control, the fewer muscle fibers controlled by a single neuron.

There are three areas of secondary motor cortex in the gyrus rostral to the primary motor cortex. Adjacent to and in front of the longitudinal fissure is the supplementary motor cortex, which is involved in planning intentional voluntary movements. Lateral to the supplementary motor cortex and extending down to the lateral fissure, the premotor cortex is involved in the control of voluntary movements in response to stimuli. The cingulate motor area is located ventral to the supplementary motor cortex inside the cingulate sulcus inside the longitudinal fissure on the medial surface of the frontal lobe.

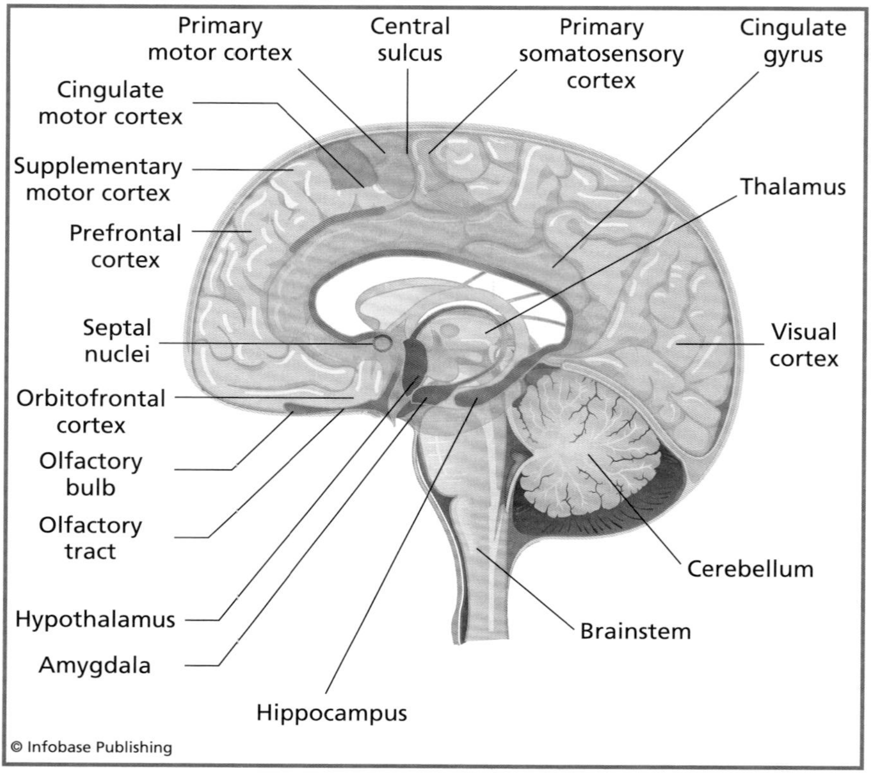

Figure 5.2 This sagittal section of the brain shows the medial portions of the primary and secondary (supplementary) motor cortices. In this view, the cingulate motor cortex and the supplementary motor cortex are visible. On the lateral aspect of the hemisphere, the supplementary motor cortex extends for a short distance and then the premotor cortex extends down to the temporal lobe.

Also considered a part of the limbic system, which is involved in the regulation of emotions, the cingulate motor area may be involved in motor responses to drives and emotions

DESCENDING PATHWAYS

Two main groups of fiber highways carry signals from the brain to the lower motor neurons. The lateral group descends through the white matter lateral to the spinal cord gray matter, whereas the ventromedial (ventral and adjacent to the midline) group travels in the ventromedial white matter of the spinal cord. The ventromedial group synapses on the motor neurons in the ventromedial gray matter, whereas the lateral group synapses on motor neurons in the lateral ventral gray matter. Neural signals that travel down the lateral pathways control and regulate voluntary movements of the limbs and extremities. Ventromedial pathways regulate posture by controlling trunk muscles and limb muscles close to the trunk.

About 1 million fibers descend together from the primary and secondary motor cortices in the **corticospinal tract (CST)**. These fibers fan out below the cortex in the corona radiata and then travel in a tract called the *internal capsule* to the midbrain. After entering the pons through the large *cerebral peduncles*, or *crus cerebri*, they break up into many small fiber bundles, which reassemble into the large fiber tract known as the *pyramid* of the medulla. Just above the juncture of the medulla and spinal cord, about 80% of these fibers cross to the opposite side of the medulla. They continue down the spinal cord as the lateral corticospinal tract. Another 10% do not cross but travel down the lateral corticospinal tract ipsilaterally. The remaining 10% travel uncrossed as the ventral corticospinal tract in the ventral or anterior white matter. They cross to the other side of the spinal cord as they reach their targets in the cervical and upper thoracic spinal cord.

Fibers of the **corticobulbar tract** leave the motor cortices and travel inside the internal capsule ventral to the corticospinal tract until they reach their targets: cranial nerve motor neurons in the brainstem and their associated interneurons in the reticular formation. Through the corticobulbar tract, the cerebral cortex exerts control over movements of the muscles of the face and head.

The other descending motor pathways start in the brainstem. Fibers of the **rubrospinal tract** begin in the red nucleus, which is located in the ventral midbrain at the same level as the superior colliculus. Rubrospinal tract fibers cross immediately to the contralateral side of the midbrain before descending through the contralateral brainstem and down the lateral white matter of the spinal cord. Fibers of the **vestibulospinal tract**, which originate in the vestibular nuclei (located in the pons and medulla), travel uncrossed down the spinal cord in the ventromedial white matter. Most fibers of the **tectospinal tract**, which begins in the superior colliculus of the midbrain, cross close to their point of origin and travel down the contralateral brainstem and the contralateral ventromedial white matter of the spinal cord. **Reticulospinal tract** fibers originate from the reticular formation in the pons and medulla. Those from the pons descend uncrossed in the ventromedial white matter of the spinal cord. Reticulospinal fibers that start in the medulla may be crossed or uncrossed and go down through the lateral white matter of the spinal cord. Scientists believe that fibers of the autonomic nervous system descend with the reticulospinal fibers.

Motor neurons in the ventrolateral spinal cord that innervate the limbs and extremities are the main targets of the fibers of the lateral corticospinal tract, which is important in independent movements of the fingers and in skilled, rapid movements of the hands. Ending primarily in the ventrolateral gray matter of the cervical spinal cord, the rubrospinal tract is thought to be important in the control of movements of hand and arm muscles but not independent finger movements. Ending on motor neurons in the ventromedial gray matter of the ipsilateral cervical and thoracic spinal cord, the ventral corticospinal tract helps control movements of the upper trunk muscles, the shoulder, and the neck.

The tectospinal tract, which projects to the cervical spinal cord, is also involved in controlling trunk, shoulder, and neck movements, especially reflexive responses to auditory, visual, and possibly somatosensory stimuli. Because the superior colliculus is important in the control of eye movements, part of the function of the tectospinal tract may be to coordinate head and eye movements. Descending primarily through the ipsilateral spinal cord, the reticulospinal tract is involved in the control of automatic movements and functions that are involved in walking and running, maintaining muscle tone and posture, sneezing, coughing, and breathing.

WHAT IS NERVE GAS?

Nerve gas is a term used for chemical warfare agents, such as sarin, that induce illness and death by their effects on neurotransmission. Most nerve agents are organophosphates—chemicals that were originally developed as, and are still widely used as, pesticides. First synthesized in 1854, widespread use of pesticides began in Germany in the 1920s. About 2,000 compounds (including tabun, sarin, and soman) were developed by German chemists as potential chemical warfare agents in the 1930s and 1940s but were never actually used in battle. Organophosphates, which are absorbed through the skin and the respiratory and digestive tracts, bind irreversibly to acetylcholinesterase, preventing the breakdown of acetylcholine in the synapse. Overstimulation of nicotinic cholinergic receptors in motor endplates causes muscle spasms, convulsions, and eventually paralysis of the muscles, including the diaphragm. Contractions of smooth muscle in the urinary tract, digestive tract, and secretory glands cause the group of cholinergic symptoms referred to as "SLUDGE": salivation, lacrimation (tear secretion), urination, diaphoresis (sweating), gastrointestinal distress (including diarrhea), and emesis (vomiting). Heart rate and respiration are also affected. Early treatment with anticholinergic drugs (such as atropine) that block cholinergic receptors and oximes (such as praloxidime) that break the bond of the nerve agent with acetylcholinesterase will avert death. Continued widespread use of organophosphates as pesticides has resulted in over 1 million cases of poisoning and 20,000 deaths per year worldwide, with the primary cause of injury and mortality being respiratory failure. Scientists believe low-level exposure to nerve gases as well as pretreatment with pyridostigmine (a reversible carbamate-type acetylcholinesterase inhibitor), together with its interactions with other prophylactic vaccines and pesticides, may have contributed to the symptoms known collectively as Gulf War Syndrome.

BASAL GANGLIA

Located at the base of the cerebral hemispheres, the basal ganglia in each hemisphere consist of the caudate nucleus, the **putamen**, the **nucleus accumbens**, the **globus pallidus**, and the **subthalamic nucleus** (Figure 5.3). Also included in the basal ganglia is a midbrain structure called the **substantia nigra**. If any of these nuclei are damaged, a person will experience severe movement problems. Among the many interconnections between the basal ganglia nuclei themselves, as well as between the basal ganglia and the thalamus and cortex, scientists have found what they refer to as four anatomical "loops."

The *skeletomotor loop* is involved with learned movements. In this loop, information from the primary motor and primary somatosensory cortices travels to the putamen. The putamen then sends the information to the globus pallidus, which projects to the ventrolateral and ventral anterior thalamic nuclei. These structures complete the loop by projecting to the primary and premotor cortices. The *prefrontal cortex loop* plays a part in the conscious planning of movements. It begins when the caudate nucleus receives information from all **association areas** (secondary and higher-order sensory areas) of the cortex. The caudate nucleus projects to the globus pallidus, which then projects to the ventral anterior thalamic nucleus. This nucleus then completes the loop by projecting to the prefrontal cortex. Information in the *limbic loop* travels from the amygdala and cingulate gyrus (both part of the limbic system) to the nucleus accumbens and from there to the globus pallidus. The globus pallidus projects to the **dorsomedial thalamic nucleus**, which in turn projects to the supplementary motor cortex and the premotor cortex. Finally, the **oculomotor loop** participates in the control of eye movements. It begins in control centers for eye movement in the frontal lobe and in higher-order visual cortex in the posterior parietal lobe. It travels from these areas to the substantia nigra, then to the ventral anterior thalamic nucleus, and finally back to the prefrontal cortex and higher-order visual areas of the frontal cortex.

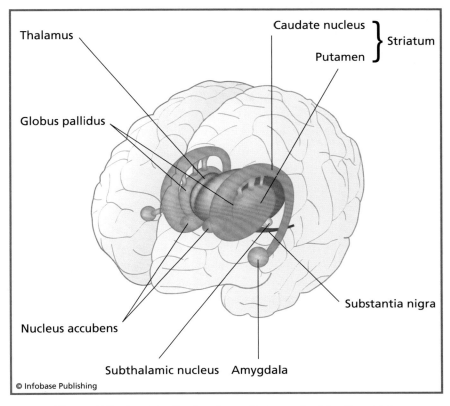

Thalamus

Caudate nucleus
Putamen
} Striatum

Globus pallidus

Substantia nigra

Nucleus accumbens

Subthalamic nucleus   Amygdala

© Infobase Publishing

Figure 5.3 Input to the basal ganglia is received by the striatum (caudate nucleus, nucleus accumbens, and putamen). After incoming information is processed, the output nuclei—the ventral pallidum, the substantia nigra, and the globus pallidus internal segment—project to thalamic nuclei, the pedunculopontine nucleus, and the superior colliculus. These output pathways control movements of the limb, trunk, eye, and facial muscles. Other basal ganglia nuclei—the subthalamic nucleus and the external segment of the globus pallidus—are part of an intrinsic basal ganglia pathway that inhibits movement production.

CEREBELLUM

Like the cerebrum, the cerebellum ("little cerebrum") has a thin, extensively folded cortex overlying a large area of white matter (Figure 5.4). Although the cerebellum is smaller than the cerebrum, its deeply folded cortex has the same amount of surface area. The 50 billion neurons in its three-layered cortex comprise more than half the neurons of the brain and outnumber the 22 billion neurons in the cerebrum. Because of its treelike appearance in the sagittal section, the white matter of the cerebellum is called the *arbor vitae* ("tree of life"). Four pairs of *deep cerebellar nuclei* lie beneath the white matter. The cerebellum is connected to the brainstem by three pairs of *cerebellar peduncles*, or large bundles of fibers. Like the cerebrum, the cerebellum has two hemispheres that are joined by a small longitudinal structure called the **vermis**. The cerebellum has deep fissures that divide it into three horizontal lobes: an anterior lobe, a posterior lobe, and the *flocculonodular lobe* at its caudal end.

Functions of the cerebellum include the coordination of all voluntary and reflex movements and the maintenance of proper muscle tone and normal body posture. Through its connections with the vestibular nuclei, the cerebellum is also involved in the maintenance of equilibrium and the control of eye movements. Cerebellar output affects primarily the ipsilateral side of the body. After receiving input from the brain and spinal cord, the neurons of the cerebellar cortex send signals to the deep cerebellar nuclei, which then send most of the cerebellum's output to other brain areas. An exception is the flocculonodular lobe, which is not connected to one of the deep cerebellar nuclei. It has direct reciprocal connections with the vestibular nuclei, through which it plays a role in equilibrium, postural reflexes, and eye movements. Vestibular input also goes to the cortex of the vermis, which signals the fastigial nucleus, which then sends an output back to the vestibular nucleus. In addition, the vermis receives auditory information from the superior colliculi, visual information from the inferior colliculi, and cutaneous and proprioreceptive information from the spinal cord. This information influences its output through the fastigial nucleus to the vestibular nucleus and to motor nuclei of cranial nerves in the

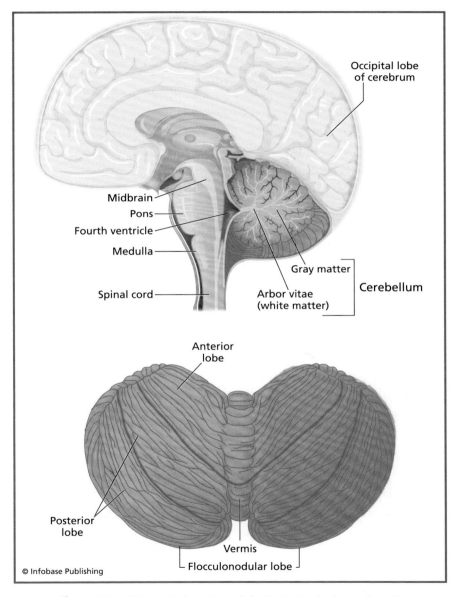

Figure 5.4 This sagittal section of the brain (*top*) shows the arbor vitae, which is the white matter of the cerebellum. The alternative view (*bottom*) shows the vermis and the anterior, middle, and posterior lobes of the cerebellum.

Clay County Public Library
116 Guffey Street
Celina, TN 38551
(931) 243-3442

reticular formation. Because of its connections, the vermis plays a role in the control of eye movements and in postural adjustments.

Somatosensory information from the spinal cord and information about intended movements from the primary motor cortex and the frontal association cortex converge in the cortex of the lateral zone. There, the optimal timing for contractions of the muscles involved in the movements is calculated. These calculations are sent to the dentate nucleus, which sends them back to the primary motor cortex through a relay in the ventrolateral thalamic nucleus. The neural signals transmitted by the corticospinal tract are influenced by these calculations. Independent limb movements are influenced by the output of the dentate nucleus to the red nucleus. Output from the intermediate zone through the emboliform and globose nuclei goes to the red nucleus and the ventrolateral nucleus of the thalamus. These connections affect the rubrospinal tract and the corticospinal tract.

Damage to different areas of the cerebellum result in different symptoms. Posture and balance are affected by damage to either the vermis or the flocculonodular lobe. Limb rigidity is the principal symptom of damage to the intermediate zone. Decomposition of movement and weakness are symptoms of damage to the lateral zone. Smooth, simultaneous movements, such as bringing one's hand to the mouth, decompose into separate movements at the wrist, elbow, and shoulder. The timing of rapid, aimed movements is also impaired by lateral zone damage and results in the overshooting of a target. Integration of movement sequences so that conscious effort is not required to make them is impaired by damage to the lateral zone.

The cerebellum is also involved in motor learning, and recent research indicates that it may be involved in higher cognitive functions as well as emotional and autonomic nervous system functions. Memory of sensorimotor tasks is now thought to be stored in the cerebellum and the striatum. Studies with neuroimaging techniques have shown that the cerebellum is activated during motor skill learning as well as during cognitive tasks such as shifting attention, mental imaging, processing language, and modulating emotion. Clinical studies of patients with cerebellar damage have found similar cognitive deficits.

Functionally, the cerebellum can be divided into three longitudinal regions: the vermix at midline, the intermediate zone on either side of the vermix, and the larger lateral zone to either side of the intermediate zone. Three fiber tracts bring information from the cerebral cortex to the cerebellum. These fiber tracts relay in brainstem structures before going through the cerebellar peduncles to the cerebellum. Somatosensory information from proprioreceptors in the tendons, muscles, and joints travels up the spinal cord to the cerebellum in three tracts. Fibers from the vestibular nucleus, the red nucleus, and the superior and inferior colliculi in the brainstem also bring information to the cerebellum.

MOTOR NEURONS

Eye muscles, facial muscles, and muscles that control the tongue, jaw, and swallowing movements are innervated by neurons found in the motor nuclei of cranial nerves. Cranial nerves exit the brainstem and travel through openings in the skull to reach their targets. The vagus nerve, which is the longest cranial nerve, travels down the neck to reach the body cavity. There, it innervates viscera of the chest and abdomen as well as the large blood vessels of the chest.

Motor neurons are also located in the ventral, or anterior, "wings" of the spinal cord gray matter. Most descending fibers actually synapse on interneurons, which then project to the motor neurons. The spinal cord has two types of motor neurons: alpha motor neurons and gamma motor neurons. **Alpha motor neurons** send commands to the extrafusal muscle fibers that cause muscles to contract. **Gamma motor neurons** are smaller than alpha motor neurons. They send signals to intrafusal muscle fibers that make muscle spindles more sensitive to external stimuli under certain conditions. Approximately 10,000 excitatory fibers from descending pathways and from proprioreceptive neurons in the dorsal horn synapse on the extensive dendritic tree of each alpha motor neuron. About 5,000 inhibitory fibers from proprioreceptive neurons synapse on the cell body. Additional inputs from nearby interneurons in the ventral gray matter may be either excitatory or inhibitory.

Motor neurons and the interneurons to which they connect are found in the spinal cord's ventral gray matter. They are arranged in clusters that activate individual muscles. Those that innervate the neck and trunk muscles are located close to the midline beneath the spinal canal. Motor neurons that innervate upper and lower limbs are located in the lateral ventral gray matter. In general, the farther the limb muscles are from the trunk, the more lateral are the neurons that innervate them. In the cervical and lumbar regions of the spinal cord, the ventral and dorsal horns ("butterfly wings") are enlarged. The motor neurons that innervate the arms and hands are found in the cervical enlargement, whereas those that innervate the legs and feet are found in the lumbar enlargement.

The synapse between an ending of an alpha motor neuron and a muscle fiber is called a **neuromuscular junction**, and the postsynaptic membrane of the synapse is a specialized area of the muscle membrane called the **muscle endplate**. Muscle endplates contain nicotinic cholinergic receptors. Each muscle fiber has one muscle endplate surrounded by a Schwann cell to keep the neurotransmitter molecules inside the synapse.

When the nicotinic cholinergic receptors are activated, an action potential called the end plate potential is generated as sodium (Na^+) ions enter channels associated with the nicotinic cholinergic receptors. This depolarizing action potential is transmitted down the length of the muscle fiber membrane and causes calcium channels in the membrane to open so that calcium ions enter the cytoplasm. Depolarization of a muscle fiber also causes calcium to be released from internal stores within the fiber. Myosin and actin are activated by the increase in calcium ions, and this results in a contraction of the muscle fiber.

TOXINS THAT AFFECT THE MOTOR NEURONS

Alpha motor neurons send collateral axons to interneurons called **Renshaw cells**. Renshaw cells send back an inhibitory signal, which helps the motor neurons to self-regulate. The neurotransmitter released by the Renshaw cell is the inhibitory neurotransmitter glycine. The bacterium *Clostridium tetani* releases tetanus toxin, a poison that prevents the release of glycine from the presynaptic terminal of Renshaw cells. Similarly, the poison strychnine blocks glycine receptors in the postsynaptic membrane of alpha motor neurons. Both toxins prevent the Renshaw cells from inhibiting the alpha motor neurons, resulting in convulsions. Because there are a large number of glycine receptors in the interneurons of the cranial nerve motor nuclei that innervate the muscles of facial expression and jaw muscles, these two toxins particularly affect these two groups of muscles. "Lockjaw," the common name for tetanitis, describes one of the symptoms of poisoning with the tetanus toxin: The teeth become clenched because of severe contractions of the jaw muscles.

In contrast, the botulinum toxin prevents the release of acetylcholine. This toxin is released by *Clostridium botulinum* and causes botulism, a type of food poisoning. Preventing the release of acetylcholine makes it impossible for the motor neurons, the autonomic preganglionic neurons, and the parasympathetic postganglionic neurons to send signals to the muscles and internal organs. The result is that the muscles of movement, the muscles of the eyelid and pupil, and the muscles of the diaphragm, urinary bladder, bowel, and salivary glands become paralyzed. People suffering from this condition often have drooping eyelids, double vision, weak limb and facial muscles, and, ultimately, paralysis of the respiratory muscles, whereby they are unable to breathe on their own.

SPINAL REFLEXES

Spinal reflexes are involuntary movements of the muscles of the trunk, limbs, and extremities that occur in response to sensory stimuli. These movements involve a circuit from one or more muscles to the spinal cord and back. The simplest reflexes involve just one sensory neuron and one motor neuron and no interneurons. These are referred to as monosynaptic reflexes. Other reflexes, called polysynaptic reflexes, involve two or more synapses, at least one of which involves an interneuron. Most reflexes are polysynaptic reflexes that may range from very simple to complex.

The only known example of the monosynaptic reflex is the stretch reflex. If a muscle fiber is stretched, a signal goes from the muscle spindle through a proprioceptive fiber that synapses on the alpha motor neuron in the spinal cord. The alpha motor neuron responds by increasing its rate of firing, which strengthens the contraction of the muscle fiber. An example of this is the knee jerk, or *patellar reflex*. When a doctor taps the patellar tendon beneath your knee with a small hammer, your thigh muscle stretches. This makes the muscle spindles fire and contract the thigh muscle, causing your lower leg to kick upward. When we lift a heavy object, the muscles in our arms increase their contractions in response to stretch, giving us the strength we need to support the weight. The stretching of the calf muscle that occurs when we lean forward causes it to contract, which allows us to maintain an upright posture.

Withdrawal reflexes, or flexor reflexes, allow us to immediately move a part of the body away from a painful stimulus by flexing the limb involved. The brainstem normally sends out signals that keep the reflex pathways somewhat inhibited. Only painful or noxious stimuli cause a strong reflexive action. Fibers from sensory neurons in the skin synapse on interneurons in the spinal cord, which, in turn, synapse on alpha motor neurons that synapse on and activate flexor muscles that move the limb away from the danger. Normally, the limb flexes to withdraw from the stimulus, but sometimes the brain has to activate the extensor muscles of another limb to withdraw it safely. A *crossed extensor reflex* involves the inhibition or activation (whichever is opposite) of the alpha motor neurons to the same muscle or group of muscles on the opposite side of the body. This allows you to alternate muscle movements during locomotion and helps maintain your posture during a withdrawal reflex. The brain can also send out signals to inhibitory interneurons to override the withdrawal reflex. Sometimes this is necessary—for example, when you need to avoid dropping a hot object you are carrying.

CONNECTIONS

About 1 million motor neurons in the spinal cord control the movements of the arms, legs, feet, hands, and trunk muscles. Neurons in cranial nerve motor nuclei perform a similar function for muscles in the head, neck, face, and eyes. Spinal and cranial nerve motor neurons are under the direct influence of neurons in the cerebral cortex and brainstem and under the indirect influence of neurons in the cerebellum. Nerve fibers descend from the cerebral cortex to cranial nerve nuclei as the corticobulbar tract and to the spinal cord as the lateral and ventral corticospinal tracts. Tracts descending to the spinal cord from the brainstem include the rubrospinal tract from the red nucleus, the vestibulospinal tract from the vestibular nucleus, the tectospinal tract from the superior colliculus, and the reticulospinal tract from the reticular formation.

The cerebellum indirectly influences the information that travels through these pathways by sending projections to the ventrolateral thalamic nuclei and to the brainstem nuclei involved. Somatosensory information that is relayed from the body via the spinal cord, as well as information that comes from the cerebral cortex and the brainstem, are processed by the cerebellum and influence its outputs. Located at the base

(continues)

(continued)

of each cerebral hemisphere, the basal ganglia nuclei have complex interconnections with each other and with the thalamus and the cerebral cortex. Some of these interconnections are involved in learning and performing motor skills and in planning movements. Others allow control of the eye movements and the involvement of drives and emotions in motor responses. Severe movement deficits result from damage to these nuclei or their interconnections. Degeneration of the dopaminergic fibers from the substantia nigra to the caudate and putamen nuclei produces the symptoms of Parkinson's disease.

6

Learning and Memory

FROM THE TIME WE TAKE OUR FIRST BREATH (AND PROBABLY even before), we are continually learning. We learn to play ball, ride a bicycle, read, write, interact with our environments, and much more. All of these learning tasks are accomplished with four basic types of learning: perceptual, stimulus-response, motor, and relational. One or more of these types is active in any given learning situation. As we learn, we form memories that help us relate newly learned information to things we have learned previously. Changes in behavior and the retrieval of information from memory are both evidence that learning has occurred.

TYPES OF LEARNING

Perceptual Learning
Perceptual learning allows us to recognize and identify stimuli we have encountered before. Changes in the higher-order cortices, or association cortex, that are associated with each of the senses allow us to recognize these stimuli when we encounter them again. Scientists believe that memories for each sensory modality are stored in a specific sensory association cortex.

Stimulus-Response Learning

Stimulus-response learning occurs when a particular response to a particular stimulus is learned. This response can be as simple as a defensive reflex or as complicated as a learned sequence of movements. Classical conditioning and instrumental conditioning are two types of stimulus-response learning. When a previously neutral stimulus is associated enough times with a stimulus that naturally produces a reflexive response, it eventually elicits the response in the absence of the original stimulus. This is known as **classical conditioning**, or **associative learning**. This type of conditioning was discovered by Russian physiologist Ivan Pavlov, who was studying salivation in dogs as part of his Nobel Prize–winning research on digestion. He discovered that the dogs he was using for research would salivate at the sight of food or even at his appearance in the room. Through experimentation, he learned that if he rang a bell each time before he fed the dogs, they would eventually salivate in response to the bell, even in the absence of food.

Instrumental conditioning occurs when we learn to associate either a reinforcement or a punishment with a particular response or behavior. This type of learning occurs, for example, in a Skinner box when a rat learns to press a lever for food or to avoid a negative stimulus, such as an electrical shock. The Skinner box was invented by American psychologist B.F. Skinner, who used the box extensively to explore instrumental conditioning. He found out, for example, that varying the number of times a rat had to press a lever to get a food pellet would affect the rate at which the rat pressed the lever. Skinner believed, correctly, that instrumental conditioning, also called *operant learning*, would work with people as well. People also will increase behaviors for which they receive positive responses and decrease behaviors for which they receive negative responses. Skinner invented "programmed instruction," in which the learner gets step-by-step feedback on the material he or she is learning.

Motor Learning

Motor learning is the learning of skilled movements, such as knitting, typing, playing the piano, riding a bicycle, or dancing. Although we make these movements slowly and deliberately when we first learn them, they become automatic with practice. As we will learn later, motor learning involves a shifting of control of the learned movements from a conscious type of memory system to an unconscious type of memory system.

Relational Learning

Relational learning involves learning relationships between multiple stimuli. It results in the formation of neural connections between the various areas of higher order sensory cortex involved. Examples of relational learning include more complex forms of perceptual learning, spatial learning, episodic learning, and observational learning. Perceptual learning that involves more than one sensory modality requires the formation of connections between the sensory association cortices involved. **Spatial learning** involves learning about the objects in the surrounding environment and their locations with respect to each other and to the learner. **Episodic learning** involves remembering events and the order, or sequence, in which they occur. **Observational learning** occurs when we learn by observing and imitating the actions of other people. In this type of learning, relationships between actions, consequences, and one's own movements must be learned.

PHASES OF MEMORY FORMATION

Learning is often defined as the process of acquiring knowledge, with memory being the end result (Figure 6.1). There are three basic aspects of memory formation: encoding, storage, and retrieval. **Encoding** is the process by which stimuli from the environment are changed into a neural code that can be perceived by the brain. **Storage**, or **consolidation**, is the process

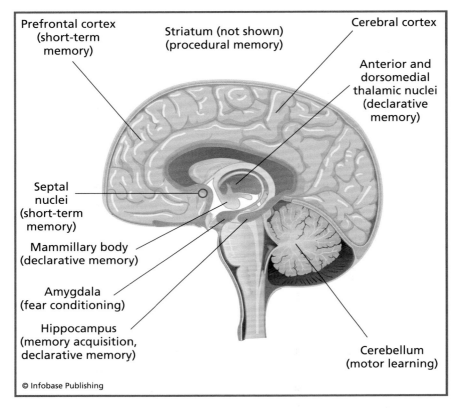

Prefrontal cortex
(short-term
memory)

Striatum (not shown)
(procedural memory)

Cerebral cortex

Anterior and
dorsomedial
thalamic nuclei
(declarative
memory)

Septal
nuclei
(short-term
memory)

Mammillary body
(declarative memory)

Amygdala
(fear conditioning)

Hippocampus
(memory acquisition,
declarative memory)

Cerebellum
(motor learning)

© Infobase Publishing

Figure 6.1　The structures that have been most strongly implicated in memory functions are shown here. Damage to these structures by disease or injury will produce a loss of memory. The memory loss of Alzheimer's disease is generally attributed to the significant damage to the hippocampus seen with that disease.

by which this encoded information is recorded in memory. **Retrieval** is the process by which information is accessed in the memory stores. Information stored in memory may be retrieved by conscious recall of specific information or by recognition of previously encountered information, such as a name, word, or place.

STAGES OF MEMORY

Before it is stored in the brain, information goes through three stages of processing. Most of the information we get

from our environment never gets beyond the first stage—
sensory memory. Sensory memory lasts only milliseconds
or seconds at most. It includes all the stimuli that come to
us from the environment. If we focus on or pay attention
to particular stimuli, that information will enter our **short-
term memory,** or **immediate memory**. This type of memory
lasts from seconds to minutes and can store seven (plus or
minus two) items. **Rehearsal**, or repetition, of the information
in short-term memory helps us keep it there longer. If the
information is important enough, it may then be transferred
into **long-term memory**, where it can remain for a lifetime.
Long-term memory has an enormous capacity. It includes all
the facts and knowledge that we accumulate throughout our
entire lives—from the rules of English grammar to the lyrics
of a favorite song.

Long-term memory includes explicit memory and implicit
memory, which, in turn, have subcategories of their own (Figure 6.2). **Explicit memory**, or **declarative memory**, is available
to the conscious mind and can be declared, or put into words.
There are two subcategories of explicit memory: episodic
memory and semantic memory. **Episodic memory**—sometimes
called personal, or autobiographical, memory—is the memory
of past experiences, or episodes, in our lives. These memories
might be as recent as what you ate for breakfast today or as far
back as your first day at elementary school. Damage to or mal-
function of the frontal lobes can result in *episodic amnesia*, the
loss of episodic memory. **Semantic memory** stores information
that is not related to a particular experience. Instead, it includes
such things as word meanings, ideas, and facts. Most of the
factual knowledge we gain in the classroom or from reading
books is stored as semantic memory.

Implicit memory, or nondeclarative memory, is stored information that is not available to conscious thought. It cannot be
put into words easily. Subcategories of implicit memory include
memories that result from classical conditioning, memories
that make priming possible, and procedural memory. Priming

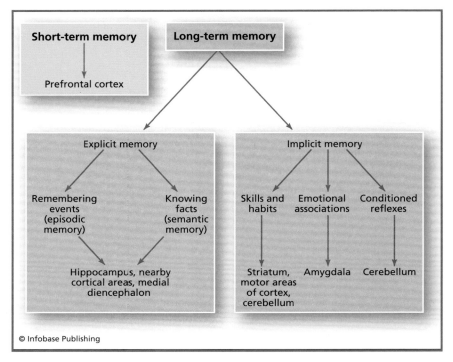

Figure 6.2 The most commonly described types of memory are depicted here with the anatomical structures with which they have been associated through research. Some of these correlations are still speculative, particularly those involving the striatum and cerebellum.

occurs when a cue such as a card containing the first three letters of a word helps us retrieve information stored in unconscious memory. **Procedural memory** includes rules, procedures, and motor skills. Sometimes they are learned unconsciously. Examples of procedural memory include learning rules of grammar or learning how to play a musical instrument.

ANATOMY OF LEARNING AND MEMORY
The Limbic System

A group of structures called the limbic system works together to produce and regulate emotions and to form new memories (Figure 6.3). There are two subsystems of the limbic system: one in which the hippocampus plays a central role and the other in which the amygdala is the key structure. The amygdala plays a key role in the regulation of emotions, and so we will discuss the second subsystem in a later section. Although it also performs other functions, the hippocampus is necessary for acquiring new memories. Scientists believe that the hippocampus is the structure where explicit memory is consolidated before it is transferred to the cerebral cortex for long-term storage. Similarly, the amygdala is involved in the consolidation of emotional memories, and the basal ganglia nuclei are involved in the consolidation of implicit memory.

The Hippocampus

Information is relayed to the hippocampus from other areas of the limbic association cortex, olfactory inputs, the amygdala, and the orbital cortex. It also receives direct projections from the septal nuclei and the hypothalamus through a large fiber bundle called the **fornix** as well as information through the **hippocampal commissure**. The hippocampal commissure is the fiber bundle that connects the two hippocampi and allows them to communicate with each other. Direct projections to the hippocampus also come from the raphe nuclei and the locus coeruleus in the brainstem, as well as from the ventral striatum. The hippocampus sends information to the subiculum, which projects back to the *entorhinal cortex*, which then sends widespread projections to the cortex.

Hippocampal output to subcortical nuclei travels through the fornix, each side of which contains more than one million axons. The fornix arches forward and downward to the mammillary bodies, which then project to the anterior thalamic nuclei, which, in turn, project to the cingulate gyrus. This completes a circuit that is involved in emotions and in learning and memory. The hippocampus also projects to the lateral septal nucleus through the fornix, which, in turn, projects to the medial septal nucleus, which then projects back through the fornix to the hippocampus.

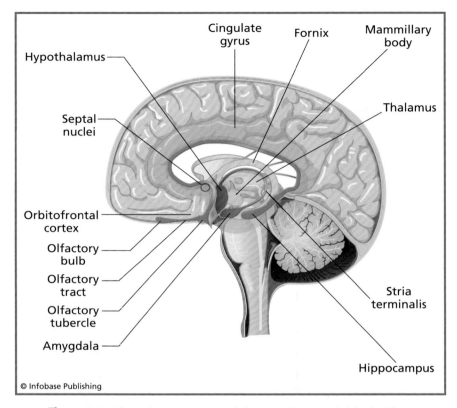

Figure 6.3 The major components of the two subsystems of the limbic system, which center around the hippocampus and the amygdala, are shown here. The subcortical components shown include the hippocampus, amygdala, hypothalamus, thalamus, and olfactory tubercle. Cortical components include the cingulate gyrus, the parahippocampal gyrus, and the orbitofrontal cortex.

Amnesia

Damage to the hippocampus or its input or output regions and fibers results in memory loss, or amnesia. Hippocampal damage can result from head trauma, aneurysms of arteries that supply the hippocampus, epileptic seizures, or loss of oxygen supply (hypoxia) during cardiac arrest. (An aneurysm is a saclike protrusion from a blood vessel that forms because the vessel wall weakens.) One of the first structures to show damage during aging or as a result of Alzheimer's disease is the hippocampus. Damage to the septal nuclei, the fornix, or the entorhinal cortex also result in amnesic symptoms.

Damage to both hippocampi results in **anterograde amnesia**, or the inability to learn new information. **Retrograde amnesia**, the loss of previously learned information, may be present as well. Loss of memory for events that occurred from 1 year up to as many as 15 years before the damage may be present in some individuals. A study published by Reed and Squire in 1998 showed that damage to the hippocampal formation alone resulted in minor retrograde amnesia. Damage to the hippocampus as well as the limbic cortex in the medial temporal lobe produced retrograde amnesia that spanned several decades.

The most famous example of anterograde amnesia is the case of a patient known as "H.M." In an attempt to stop his epileptic seizures, about 2 inches of H.M.'s medial temporal lobe (including the amygdala), about two-thirds of the hippocampus, and the overlying cortex were surgically removed on each side (Figure 6.4). From the time of the operation, which occurred in 1953, scientists studied H.M. continually. Although he could store new information temporarily in his short-term memory, he could no longer form any new long-term memories. Rehearsal of information in his short-term memory allowed him to hold onto information until he was distracted, at which point he lost the memory. In contrast to his inability to form new memories, H.M.'s retrograde memory loss was limited to a period of 11 years before his surgery at age 27. His memories formed before age 16 were still intact. Although H.M. learned and retained motor skills, he could not remember having learned them or having performed them.

Studies in animals and in human patients like H.M. have shown that damage to the hippocampus causes problems in explicit memory but not in implicit memory. This suggests that there may be multiple memory systems within the brain. Free recall of information as well as recognition memory (the ability

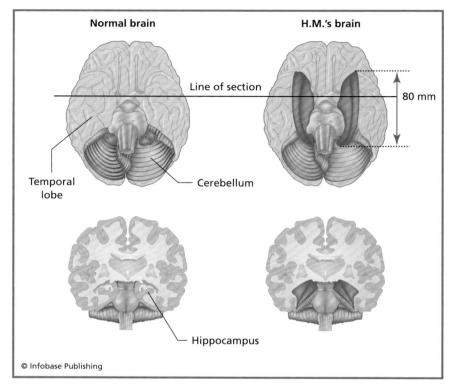

Normal brain

H.M.'s brain

Line of section

80 mm

Temporal
lobe

Cerebellum

Hippocampus

© Infobase Publishing

Figure 6.4   The upper right figure shows the areas of the medial temporal lobe that were removed on both sides of H. M.'s brain. This view is of the ventral, or undersurface, of the brain. The horizontal line across the two upper figures shows where the brain would be cut to produce the sections shown in the two lower figures. In the lower right figure, you can see that the hippocampus and overlying cortex are missing. The two figures on the left show a normal brain for comparison.

to recall previously encountered information) are impaired after hippocampal damage. Neuroimaging studies that use memory tasks in humans have shown that the hippocampus is active during both the formation and retrieval of memories. Most scientists currently believe that the hippocampus processes the information it receives from cortical association areas and from subcortical areas, such as the amygdala and basal ganglia, and then sends messages back to these areas that modify the way the components of a memory are stored. In these memories, individual components are linked together so that they can be retrieved as a complete memory.

Midline Diencephalic Nuclei

Damage to diencephalic structures adjacent to the third ventricle, such as the midthalamic nuclei and the mammillary bodies, also causes amnesia. Korsakoff's syndrome, which is usually caused by severe thiamine deficiency resulting from years of alcohol abuse, results in damage to the mammillary bodies and other structures. One of the symptoms of Korsakoff's syndrome is anterograde amnesia. Strokes that affect the thalamus can also cause amnesia. Amnesia resulting from damage to these diencephalic structures probably occurs because of their connections to other structures, such as the hippocampus and the frontal cortex.

Prefrontal Cortex

Areas in the frontal cortex appear to be involved in planning, problem solving, and producing organizational strategies used in memory tasks. Results of neuroimaging studies have suggested that the left inferior (lower) prefrontal cortex is important in encoding information for storage and in conceptual processing, or processing related to the meaning of words. Other neuroimaging studies have shown that an area of the right prefrontal cortex is involved in retrieving memories. Studies of patients with frontal lobe damage and neuroimaging studies of frontal lobe activity have shown that the frontal lobes are involved in holding onto the information we need for ongoing tasks in short-term or working memory. There is increased activation of the prefrontal cortex during working memory tasks, such as remembering a phone number long enough to dial it.

Basal Ganglia and Cerebellum

Research suggests that once learned skills become automatic (when we can perform them without thinking about them consciously), control of these behaviors is transferred from the sensory and motor association cortices to the basal ganglia. The caudate and putamen nuclei get information about movements from the motor areas of the frontal cortex. They also receive sensory information from all cortical regions. Outputs of the caudate and putamen nuclei go to the globus pallidus, which sends information to the ventrolateral and ventral anterior thalamic nuclei. As these thalamic nuclei relay the information to the primary, premotor, and supplementary motor cortices, the skeletomotor loop is completed. Projections from the globus pallidus also travel to the dorsomedial thalamic nucleus, which projects to cognitive areas of the frontal lobe.

Laboratory animals with damage to the basal ganglia have problems with instrumental conditioning. People who suffer from Huntington's disease or Parkinson's disease, which involve degenerative damage to the basal ganglia, experience both cognitive and motor problems. Patients with Parkinson's disease show slowness of thought, have a hard time switching from one task to another, and have difficulty interpreting nonverbal social cues ("body language"). Patients with Huntington's disease have even more severe cognitive impairment and frequently suffer from dementia.

Another loop goes from the motor cortex to the cerebellum and back to the cortex by way of the thalamus. This loop also appears to play a role in motor skill learning. Activity in both loops has been observed during neuroimaging studies of motor learning. The cerebellum seems to be most involved when we are learning a motor skill. As we practice the task, the cerebellum's involvement decreases. By the time the practiced skill becomes automatic, the involvement of the cerebellum can no longer be detected. However, basal ganglia involvement appears to be greatest after the skill becomes automatic, and it does not decrease after that point.

Motor Association Cortex

Given the involvement of the premotor and supplementary cortices in motor planning and the fact that they are the target of most of the information relayed from the basal ganglia through the thalamus, it would be reasonable to assume that the motor association cortex is involved in motor learning. Research has shown that damage to the supplementary motor cortex impairs self-initiated movements and the performance of a sequence of movements. A positron emission tomography, or PET (a type of neuroimaging), study in humans backed up this observation by demonstrating that the supplementary motor cortex is activated during the learning and performance of a sequence of movements. Some scientists believe that memories are stored in the sensory association cortices associated with the different senses and in the areas involved in the performance of a particular task. If these scientists are correct, then the motor association cortex, along with the cerebellum and the basal ganglia, would be among the places where motor learning information is most likely to be stored.

Amygdala

Memory consolidation is enhanced by epinephrine (adrenaline) and glucocorticoids (cortisol), which are stress hormones released by the adrenal glands. Research indicates that stress hormones cause the amygdala's basolateral nucleus to release norepinephrine. (Epinephrine also causes the liver to release glucose, the primary fuel of the brain.) In experimental animals, a mild shock to the feet as well as certain drugs that enhance the consolidation of memory also increase the release of norepinephrine in the basolateral nucleus. Activation of one cholinergic receptor subtype in the basolateral amygdala appears to be important for the effects of glucocorticoids on memory consolidation enhancement. Some scientists think the amygdala may be the site where the neural changes that produce learned fear occur. But most research indicates that the role of the amygdala in memory consolidation is a modulatory one that affects other brain areas.

PHYSIOLOGY OF LEARNING AND MEMORY

Learning and memory processes produce synaptic changes in the neural circuits that they activate. Studies have shown that the brains of rats raised in an enriched environment—where they had access to other rats, slides, ladders, running wheels, and toys—weighed more and had a thicker cortex, more glial cells, a better blood supply, and larger postsynaptic areas than rats raised alone in a cage with no external stimulation. In one study, rats that were exposed to the extensive visual stimulation of training in a maze series had larger dendritic trees on the neurons in their visual cortex.

LONG-TERM POTENTIATION

Processes such as long-term potentiation (LTP) may be responsible for some synaptic changes. LTP is the strengthening, or **potentiation**, of a synapse as a result of high-frequency stimulation. Although not all scientists agree, many do believe that LTP is a necessary process in memory consolidation. If a stimulating microelectrode is placed in the perforant pathway from the entorhinal cortex to the dentate gyrus and a recording microelectrode is placed near the dentate gyrus granule cells, the population, or group, excitatory postsynaptic potential (EPSP) of those neurons can be measured as they are stimulated. To obtain a baseline, or control measurement, the population EPSP is measured after the pathway is stimulated with a single pulse of electricity. Then a series of electrical impulses is transmitted through the perforant pathway to the granule cells. As few as 100 such impulses delivered in a period of a few seconds will produce an increase (*potentiation*) of the population EPSP that will last for weeks to months (*long-term*). This strengthening of synaptic function by LTP occurs not only in the glutamatergic pathways of the hippocampus but also in other brain areas, including the amygdala, the prefrontal cortex, the thalamus, the entorhinal cortex, the visual cortex, and the cerebellum. Strengthening of the synapses by LTP involves the synthesis of a variety of proteins, some of which are involved in the growth of dendritic spines and the enlargement of postsynaptic areas.

LONG-TERM DEPRESSION

Another process, called long-term depression (LTD), which is also present in multiple brain areas, has an effect opposite that of LTP. A low level of stimulation produces LTD. In the laboratory, this can be simulated by transmitting electrical impulses of lower frequency through glutamatergic pathways. LTD may be important in the extinction of learned responses when they are no longer useful.

COGNITIVE REHABILITATION THERAPY

Cognitive rehabilitation therapy is designed to restore or compensate for cognitive functions lost due to stroke, trauma, disease, tumor, or deficits in brain development. A neuropsychologist, physical therapist, or speech therapist usually conducts this type of therapy. Vision therapists also offer therapy for visual memory and visual perception problems. A number of computer programs have been designed for use both in the therapist's office and at home. The activities and computer programs improve or strengthen memory, visual perception, attention, learning skills, cognitive processing speed, problem solving and reasoning, abstract and critical thinking, and impulse control. Feuerstein's Instrumental Enrichment program is a related type of therapy that emphasizes the idea of "cognitive modifiability." This concept is based on the belief that intelligence is not fixed, but can be modified. Thinking skills are taught with a series of tasks that gradually become more complex and abstract. This program has not only been used clinically but is also being used in classrooms to help students "learn how to learn."

CONNECTIONS

Learning allows us to recognize environmental stimuli and their relationships to each other and to respond to them appropriately. It also helps us develop skilled behaviors that let us interact with our environment. Learned information is stored in memory for future use. Important stimuli from the environment are encoded from immediate memory into short-term memory, which has limited storage capacity. Information that is important enough or has been rehearsed can be put into long-term memory, which has a very large storage capacity. Explicit memory, but not implicit memory, is accessible to conscious thought processes. Semantic and episodic memory—remembering facts and events, respectively—are forms of explicit memory. Memories that are formed through conditioning and motor learning, as well as the learning of rules, are examples of implicit memory. Structures of the limbic system, particularly the hippocampus, are believed to be involved in the processes that underlie learning and memory. Areas in the prefrontal cortex also appear to be involved in helping the brain organize memory tasks, encoding and retrieving information, and holding information in working memory. Basal ganglia structures and the cerebellum are important for motor-skill learning and possibly other cognitive functions. Emotional memories may be consolidated in the amygdala.

7

Emotions and Reward Systems

YOU MIGHT SAY THAT EMOTIONS ADD THE "FLAVOR" TO LIFE'S activities and the "color" to our memories. Depending on the situation, they can lift us to the heights of exhilaration or plunge us into the depths of despair. Most of our emotions, however, lie somewhere between these two extremes. What most of us do not realize is that the feelings that accompany these emotions are powered by physiological changes that are put into motion by the central nervous system. In this section, we will take a look at the brain structures involved in both positive and negative emotions and the neural connections that allow the integration of the psychological and physiological components of emotion.

NEUROANATOMY OF EMOTIONS

Just as the hippocampus is the central structure in memory formation, the amygdala is the major structure in the creation and expression of emotions. Like the hippocampus, the amygdala has both direct and indirect interconnections with the cerebral cortex. Both the amygdala and the hippocampus also have direct connections to the hypothalamus and indirect connections to the thalamus.

THE AMYGDALA

Scientists disagree on how to group the nuclei of the amygdala. Some say two groups (basolateral and corticomedial), some say three (basolateral, central, and corticomedial), and some say four, as shown in Figure 7.1. Research has shown that the baso-lateral nuclei give a stimulus emotional significance. Sensory information goes to the basolateral amygdala from all areas of the secondary and higher-order sensory cortices. After pro-cessing this information, the basolateral amygdala sends direct projections to the prefrontal cortex, the hippocampus, and the limbic association cortex. Indirect projections from the baso-lateral amygdala to the cortex are sent by way of medial dorsal thalamic, septal, and central amygdala nuclei.

The basolateral amygdala is also part of the limbic loop, which begins in the ventral striatum (nucleus accumbens), an area that has direct reciprocal connections with the amygdala. Information from the hippocampus, the limbic association cortex, and all four divisions of the amygdala arrives in the nucleus accumbens, which processes this information and sends its output to the ventral globus pallidus. From there it passes to the medial dorsal thalamic nucleus and then to the prefrontal cortex, the anterior cingulate gyrus, and the medial orbitofrontal cortex. These areas then project to the premotor cortex, which, in turn, projects to the primary motor cortex for the execution of movements.

The emotional response consists of both physiological (autonomic and hormonal) and behavioral components. It is regulated by the central nuclei, which play a role in the control of the autonomic nervous system. Sensory informa-tion from the cortex is relayed through the basolateral nuclei to the central nuclei. Emotional learning associated with aversive (unpleasant) stimuli is also modulated by the cen-tral nuclei, which, studies have shown, is necessary for the conditioned emotional response (CER) task. CER is a learn-ing task in which animals exhibit fear after being trained to

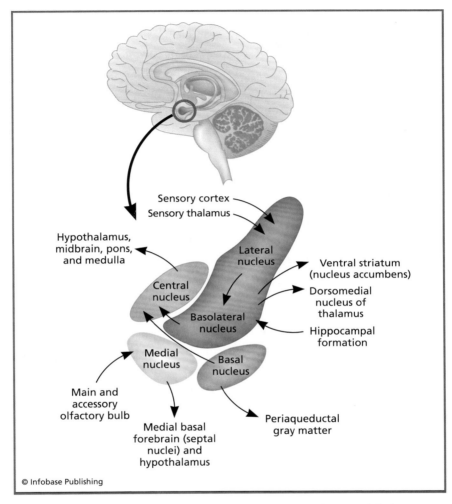

Figure 7.1 Some scientists divide the nuclei of the amygdala into four groups. The lateral/basolateral nuclei have direct reciprocal connections with higher-order sensory cortices and the hippocampus and also send relays to the cortex through the thalamus and basal forebrain. Sensory information received by the basal nuclei from the lateral/basolateral nuclei is relayed to the periaqueductal gray matter and to other amygdaloid nuclei. The central nuclei receive information from the lateral/basolateral nuclei and from the brainstem and project to the lateral hypothalamus and the brainstem to regulate the autonomic nervous system. Medial nuclei receive primary olfactory information and relay it to the hypothalamus and medial basal forebrain.

associate a tone or other stimulus with an aversive stimulus, such as a mild electrical shock to the feet. Outputs from the central nuclei to the lateral hypothalamus trigger the characteristic physiological responses of fear. These include an increase in blood pressure, the activation of the sympathetic nervous system, and the production of stress hormones by the adrenal glands. Input to the paraventricular nucleus of the hypothalamus from the central nuclei is important in control of neuroendocrine functions. There are also outputs from the hypothalamus and central nuclei to the midbrain **periaqueductal gray area**, which surrounds the cerebral aqueduct and mediates species-specific motor responses, such as hissing and growling, to emotional stimuli. The central nuclei, as well as the basolateral nuclei, are also important in addiction and substance abuse.

One of the areas to which the olfactory bulb projects is the corticomedial nuclei. Sexual behaviors, which are thought to be triggered in animals by olfactory stimuli, are regulated to some extent by the corticomedial amygdala. Through its projection to the ventromedial hypothalamic nucleus, the corticomedial amygdala is also involved in influencing feeding behavior.

There are two major output pathways from the amygdala: the **stria terminalis** and the **amygdalofugal pathway**. Most of the fibers in the stria terminalis go to and from the corticomedial nuclei. In its descent to the hypothalamic ventromedial nucleus (its primary target), the stria terminalis follows a C-shaped path along the caudate nucleus and lateral ventricle. Fibers also pass from one amygdala to the other through the stria terminalis and then across the **anterior commissure**. The **bed nucleus of the stria terminalis** follows the course of the fiber pathway and has projections and functions similar to those of the central nuclei. Most of the fibers that course through the amygdalofugal pathway go to and from the basolateral and central nuclear divisions. There are also fibers that connect the amygdalar nuclei to other structures without passing through these two major fiber pathways.

Like other major structures of the limbic system (including the hippocampus), the amygdala receives projections from dopaminergic, serotonergic, and adrenergic nuclei in the brainstem, as well as the cholinergic septal nuclei through the median forebrain bundle. This is an important fiber pathway through which fibers from each of these neurotransmitter systems travel.

THE FRONTAL LOBES

Although the amygdala is important in evaluating emotional significance and generating involuntary behavioral, autonomic, and neuroendocrine responses to stimuli, the frontal lobes are involved in the conscious experience of emotions and in controlling emotional behavior. Located on the underside of each cerebral hemisphere (just above the bones of the eye sockets), the **orbitofrontal cortex** is the part of the frontal lobe that appears to be most directly involved in emotions.

THE STRANGE STORY OF PHINEAS GAGE

An unusual case illustrates very clearly just how important the frontal lobes are. In 1848, a 25-year-old construction worker named Phineas Gage was injured in an explosion while on the job. A 3-foot-long metal rod shot up through Gage's skull. Miraculously, he survived. However, the people who knew him quickly noticed some major changes in his personality. Before the accident, Gage had been friendly and hardworking. After the injury to the frontal lobes of his brain, though, he suddenly became ornery, loud, and unstable in his moods. Scientists today know that the area of Gage's brain that was damaged—the prefrontal cortex—is responsible for regulating emotions. Because this part of his brain could no longer function, Gage had no real control over his feelings and impulses. Gage was left unable to return to his construction job. After the accident, he primarily worked in livery stables and drove coaches, and he also made an appearance at P.T. Barnum's museum in New York.

In a surgical procedure known as **prefrontal lobotomy**, the fiber pathways to and from the frontal lobes, mainly those to and from the orbitofrontal cortex, are disconnected from the rest of the brain to relieve emotional distress. Egas Moniz, the Portuguese neuropsychiatrist who introduced the procedure in the late 1930s, received a Nobel Prize for Physiology or Medicine in 1949 for developing this procedure. In some of the surgeries performed as the procedure became popular, the ventral connections of the frontal lobes with the temporal lobes and diencephalon were cut. In others, dorsal connections were severed between the frontal lobes and the cingulate gyrus. Unfortunately, the procedure eliminated both pathological reactions *and* normal emotional reactions. Though intellectual ability was not harmed by the operation, patients developed serious personality changes. They often became childish and irresponsible, were unable to carry out plans, and were usually left unemployable. Thousands of these surgeries were done before the procedure was finally abandoned because of its harmful side effects.

REWARD MECHANISMS

Natural reinforcers (such as food, water, and sex) stimulate the "pleasure centers" of the brain. So, too, do addictive drugs—including cocaine, amphetamines, cannabis, heroin, morphine, alcohol, nicotine, and caffeine. These natural and artificial reinforcers increase the release of the neurotransmitter dopamine in the nucleus accumbens. The nucleus accumbens is the site where the caudate and putamen nuclei fuse. It is sometimes referred to as the ventral striatum. The dopamine released in the nucleus accumbens is synthesized by dopaminergic neurons that project to the nucleus accumbens from the ventral tegmental area (VTA) in the midbrain. These dopaminergic fibers travel through the median forebrain bundle to the nucleus accumbens, as well as to the amygdala and the prefrontal cortex. Glutamatergic projections from the prefrontal cortex, basolateral amygdala, and hippocampus also synapse on nucleus accumbens neurons.

There are a number of "pleasure centers" in the brain for which rats will press a lever to receive electrical stimulation through an electrode implanted there. Rats will press longest and hardest for stimulation of the median forebrain bundle, especially where it crosses the lateral hypothalamus. A rat will press the lever at a high rate for hours and neglect to eat or drink, preferring instead to obtain electrical stimulation through the electrode planted there. In the median forebrain bundle are found serotonergic and adrenergic fibers in addition to the dopaminergic fibers. However, when the rats are given drugs that block dopaminergic receptors—but not when they are given those that block serotonergic or adrenergic receptors—they reduce or even stop their lever-pressing for self-stimulation.

One characteristic that addictive drugs have in common is their ability to increase the release of dopamine in the nucleus accumbens. Cocaine increases the amount of dopamine, serotonin, and norepinephrine in a synapse by blocking their reuptake into the presynaptic terminal by their respective transporters. Amphetamines act to block reuptake and to increase the release of neurotransmitters. Caffeine stimulates dopamine release by blocking adenosine receptors, which inhibit dopamine release. Marijuana contains a substance called tetrahydrocannibol (THC) that binds to the cannaboid receptors, which are the sites where the endogenous (internally produced) cannaboids anandamide and 2-arachidonoyl activate the VTA dopaminergic neurons. Binding to presynaptic nicotinic receptors, nicotine increases the excitatory effects of glutamatergic projections to the VTA and decreases the inhibitory effects of GABAergic projections. Opiates bind to opioid receptors on the presynaptic terminals of GABAergic neurons and inhibit the release of gamma-amino butyric acid (GABA). Ethanol (alcohol) binds to and blocks GABA receptors on the dendrites of the postsynaptic dopaminergic neuron. Preventing the release of GABA from presynaptic terminals or blocking its effects on postsynaptic receptors results in a disinhibition of the dopaminergic neurons and the subsequent increase in the release of dopamine.

An increase in dopamine in the nucleus accumbens by natural reinforcers fulfills natural drives that promote health and well-being (Figure 7.2). Just as the amygdala is important in enhancing memories associated with negative stimuli, the nucleus accumbens helps reinforce memories associated with positive, or pleasurable, stimuli. Like the amygdala, the nucleus accumbens also acts as an interface between the emotional components of the limbic system and the behavioral-activating components of the motor system. Once positive or negative emotions have been associated with a stimulus, the prefrontal cortex chooses appropriate behavioral reactions, which the motor system carries out.

Addictive drugs cause abnormally large increases in dopamine release in the nucleus accumbens and the prefrontal cortex. With continued use of the drug, the high levels of dopamine cause changes in the density of dopaminergic receptors in the synapses, changes in other cellular mechanisms, and even changes in synaptic connections similar to those seen in learning and memory. When there is not enough of the drug in the brain to fill the available receptors, the drug user experiences withdrawal symptoms. Similar to the takeover of a cell's DNA machinery by a virus, the reward system has in effect been commandeered by the addictive drug and now serves to increase consumption of the drug in preference to natural drives. Instead of promoting health and well being, the reward system has spun out of control in a pathway that leads to disease and even death.

Emotional memories, which are remembered more easily and for a longer period of time than other memories, involve the association of emotions with stimuli. Some scientists believe that there is a memory component of drug craving that

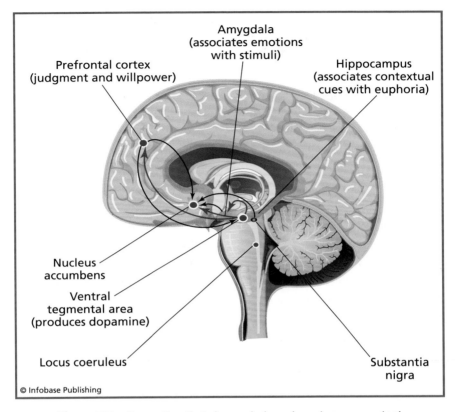

Prefrontal cortex
(judgment and willpower)

Amygdala
(associates emotions
with stimuli)

Hippocampus
(associates contextual
cues with euphoria)

Nucleus
accumbens

Ventral
tegmental area
(produces dopamine)

Locus coeruleus

Substantia
nigra

© Infobase Publishing

Figure 7.2   One action that drugs of abuse have in common is the stimulation of an increase in release of dopamine from neurons of the VTA that synapse in the nucleus accumbens. Some addictive drugs have actions in other brain structures as well. Depicted here are the basic dopaminergic pathways from the VTA to the nucleus accumbens, prefrontal cortex, and amygdala.

is produced by the association of the euphoria produced by the drug with people, places, and paraphernalia present when the drug was taken. Memory formation and drug addiction have a number of things in common: circuitry in the limbic system, changes in synaptic plasticity involving LTP and LTD, and certain intracellular mechanisms. Drug addiction, therefore, may in some respects be considered a maladaptive form of learning and memory.

ALBERT AND THE WHITE RAT: CONDITIONED EMOTIONAL RESPONSE

A conditioned emotional response is actually a learned response in which a previously neutral stimulus becomes associated with a stimulus that naturally produces a pleasant or an unpleasant emotion. The most famous (or notorious) example can be found in the results of a series of experiments published by John B. Watson and his graduate student, Rosalie Rayner, in 1920. The study is often referred to as "Albert and the White Rat." Albert, a placid 9-month-old boy, was shown several items, including a white rat, a dog, a rabbit, a monkey, burning newspapers, and masks (some with hair). He did not react with fear to any of them. Subsequently, Watson and Rayner made a loud sound by striking a steel bar suspended behind Albert's head with a hammer. For the first time, Albert showed a fear response. Later, the researchers brought out the white rat again, and struck the bar with the hammer as Albert reached for the rat. Albert gradually became conditioned to fear the white rat and the other animals from the series of experiments that followed. His fear conditioning was still apparent at the age of one year, when Albert was tested with a Santa Claus mask, fur coat, white rat, rabbit, and dog. Unfortunately, the researchers lost contact with Albert, and never got the chance to extinguish his fear of the items. One of the conclusions that Watson and Rayner drew from this experiment was that phobias may be the result of fear conditioning that takes place at some point in one's life.

Scientists today continue to use the conditioned emotional response in animal research, typically using a Skinner box, where a stimulus, such as a tone, is paired a number of times with a brief footshock and then alone during testing the following day. The physiological and behavioral responses elicited by the footshock alone before conditioning are elicited by the tone alone after conditioning. These responses include freezing behavior (ceasing lever-pressing or other ongoing behavior) and an increase in blood pressure, both of which can be eliminated by a lesion of the central amygdala. Of course, pleasant emotions can be and are paired with various stimuli during our daily lives, and many pleasant and unpleasant associations are made without our conscious awareness, therefore influencing our behavior.

CONNECTIONS

Emotional significance is associated with stimuli by the basolateral amygdala. Physiological components of emotional responses are regulated by the central amygdala through its regulation of the autonomic nervous system by projections to the hypothalamus, parasympathetic brainstem nuclei, and the reticular formation. Behavioral components of emotional responses are regulated through the involvement of the basolateral nucleus in the basal ganglia limbic loop and through projections from the central nucleus directly to the periaqueductal gray matter and indirectly to the reticular formation via the hypothalamus. The most important frontal lobe structure involved in emotions is the orbitofrontal cortex.

Reward, or pleasure, pathways in the brain involve the dopaminergic projections from the VTA to the nucleus accumbens and the prefrontal cortex. Addictive drugs have in common their ability to stimulate the release of dopamine in the nucleus accumbens through stimulation or disinhibition of dopaminergic neurons in the VTA. Learning and addiction both involve limbic system circuitry, certain intracellular mechanisms, and changes in synaptic plasticity. There appears to be a reward component as well as an associative learning component of addiction.

8

Neuroendocrine and Neuroimmune Interactions

THE HYPOTHALAMUS AND THE ENDOCRINE SYSTEM

THE HYPOTHALAMUS IS THE PRIMARY REGULATOR OF THE endocrine system and autonomic nervous system—no small task for a structure that weighs only 4 grams, or 0.3% of the weight of the entire brain! Forming the lower walls and the floor of the third ventricle in the diencephalon, the paired hypothalami are situated just below and anterior to the thalamus and just above the optic chiasm and tracts. The ventral surface of the hypothalamus forms the area at the base of the brain known as the tuber cinerium, from which protrudes the median eminence. The infundibular stalk protrudes from the median eminence and ends in the posterior lobe of the pituitary gland.

Direct cortical projections from the medial prefrontal cortex, the insular cortex, the orbital cortex, the cingulate gyrus, and other areas of the cortex travel through the median forebrain bundle to hypothalamic nuclei. Some of the serotinergic, noradrenergic, and dopaminergic fibers that also travel through the median forebrain bundle terminate on hypothalamic nuclei.

Input to the hypothalamic nuclei travels in the median forebrain bundle from the septal nuclei, in the fornix from the hippocampus, and in the stria terminalis as well as by a shorter direct pathway from the amygdala. Thalamic fibers from the midline and medial thalamic nuclei also project to the hypothalamus. Sensory information from the sense organs and the internal body organs (viscera) reaches the hypothalamus from the spinal cord and from brainstem nuclei. There is a direct projection to the **suprachiasmatic nucleus (SCN)** from the retina.

Most of the structures that send projections to the hypothalamus receive projections from the hypothalamus over the same pathways. However, there are a few pathways that are primarily output pathways from the hypothalamus. These include the *mammillothalamic tract,* which projects to the anterior thalamic nucleus from the mammillary body, and the *mammillotegmental tract*, a branch of the mammillothalamic tract that projects to the reticular formation in the midbrain. There are also histaminergic and neuropeptide pathways from hypothalamic nuclei, which are primarily output pathways.

THE HYPOTHALAMUS AND THE PITUITARY GLAND

Hypothalamic control of the pituitary gland is exerted through neural output to the posterior lobe of the pituitary gland and through a vascular pathway to the anterior lobe. Neurosecretory cells in the paraventricular and supraoptic nuclei of the hypothalamus produce the hormones **vasopressin** and **oxytocin**, which are released into the posterior lobe from axon terminals. (This means that, unlike the anterior pituitary, the posterior pituitary is actually part of the brain.) Once in the bloodstream, vasopressin, also known as **antidiuretic hormone (ADH)**, helps regulate kidney function (Figure 8.1). It causes the kidney to reabsorb more water and decrease urine production. Vasopressin also increases blood pressure by causing the smooth muscle of blood vessels to contract. Oxytocin causes smooth muscles in the uterus and mammary glands to contract. Its action brings on the contractions of childbirth

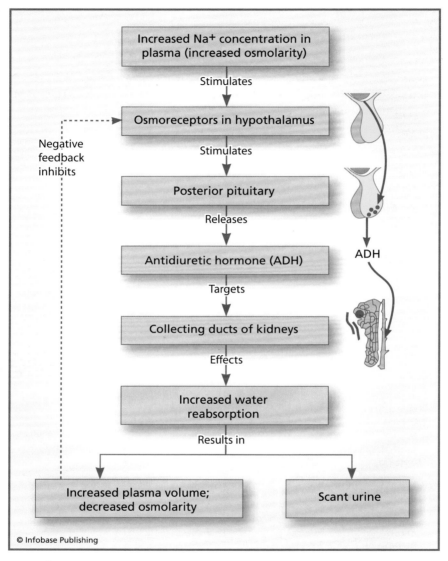

Figure 8.1 Antidiuretic hormone (ADH), or vasopressin, is released by axons from the hypothalamus into the posterior pituitary, from which it enters the bloodstream. Drinking too much water causes a decrease in the secretion of ADH. Dehydration causes an increase in ADH secretion, which causes the kidneys to retain more fluid. The process of ADH release and its effects on water retention and elimination are illustrated here.

and the release of milk during breastfeeding. Table 8.1 lists some of the most important hormones of the hypothalamus and the effects they have on the body.

The hypothalamus controls the release of hormones from the anterior lobe, or **adenohypophysis**, through its blood supply. Small peptides called hypothalamic-releasing and inhibitory hormones are released from the axon terminals of several hypothalamic nuclei near a capillary bed in the median

TABLE 8.1 SOME IMPORTANT HYPOTHALAMIC HORMONES

HORMONE	SITE OF SYNTHESIS	FUNCTION
Corticotropin-releasing hormone production (CRH)	Paraventricular nucleus Arcuate nucleus Dorsomedial nucleus	Stimulates adrenocorticotropic hormone (ACTH) production (triggers hypothalamic-pituitary-adrenal [HPA] axis)
Dopamine	Arcuate nucleus Periventricular nucleus	Inhibits thyroid-stimulating hormone (TSH) and growth-hormone (GH) release
Growth hormone releasing-hormone (GHRH)	Arcuate nucleus Perifornical area	Stimulates release of GH
Gonadotropin-releasing hormone (GNRH)	Preoptic area Arcuate nucleus Periventricular nucleus Suprachiasmatic area	Stimulates release of gonadotropins*—follicle-stimulating hormone (FSH) and luteinizing hormone (LH)
Oxytocin	Paraventricular nucleus Supraoptic nucleus	Causes smooth muscle contraction for childbirth and milk ejection
Somatostatin	Arcuate nucleus Dorsomedial nucleus	Inhibits TSH and GH release
Thyrotropin-releasing hormone (TRH)	Paraventricular nucleus (mostly) Perifornical area Suprachiasmatic nucleus (SCN)	Stimulates release of TSH
Vasopressin	Paraventricular nucleus Supraoptic nucleus	Causes kidney to reabsorb water; prevents dehydration
* FSH causes ovarian follicle development, and LH causes ovulation.		

eminence and the adjacent portion of the infundibular stalk. Hypophyseal portal vessels, which these capillaries drain into, course through the infundibular stalk into the anterior lobe of the pituitary, where they empty into sinusoids (highly permeable small blood vessels), which supply the hormone-producing cells of the pituitary. Through their actions on pituitary cells, releasing hormones increase the production of pituitary hormones; inhibiting hormones have the opposite effect.

Close to 40 neuropeptides are released by hypothalamic nuclei into the median eminence area before entering the circulatory system en route to the pituitary. In addition to the releasing and inhibiting hormones, peptides synthesized by hypothalamic neurons include growth factors, neurotensin, endogenous opiates, orexins, galanin, delta sleep-inducing peptide, substance P, and peptides that either stimulate or inhibit feeding. Among these peptides, neuropeptide Y is the most potent stimulator of food intake. In addition to other functions, orexins and galanin also stimulate food intake. Neuropeptide hormones that are not releasing factors enter the general circulation and travel to their sites of action.

THE HYPOTHALAMUS AND HOMEOSTASIS

Thermoreceptors in the hypothalamus detect changes in body temperature and send nerve signals to the autonomic nervous system. Activation of the autonomic nervous system produces the behavioral and physiological changes that are needed to adapt to the temperature of the environment. Projections to the autonomic nervous system from the preoptic area and anterior hypothalamus produce increased sweating and vasodilation to let off heat. In animals, projections to the somatic motor system cause panting. Activation of the autonomic nervous system by the posterior hypothalamus causes shivering to produce heat and **vasoconstriction** to conserve heat.

Osmoreceptors in the hypothalamus detect changes in the concentration of certain substances, such as sodium, in the blood (blood **osmolarity**). Drinking too much water makes osmolarity decrease, whereas dehydration causes an increase in osmolarity. When osmolarity rises, it triggers a release of vasopressin. Decreases in osmolarity cause a reduction in vasopressin secretion, resulting in more water being excreted by the kidneys. Vasopressin secretion can also be activated by stress, pain, and certain emotional states.

THE HYPOTHALAMUS AND INGESTIVE BEHAVIOR

If the lateral area of the hypothalamus is damaged, food and water intake—and, consequently, body weight—decrease. Neurons in the lateral hypothalamus produce and release orexin and melanin-concentrating hormone, which influence feeding behavior. Diverse projections from these neurons may influence cortical areas involved in feeding behavior. Norepinephrine release from the paraventricular nucleus also stimulates eating behavior, particularly of carbohydrates. It is not known whether this is a direct effect or an indirect effect through the increase in insulin that it causes. Galanin, a neuropeptide that is co-released with norepinephrine, stimulates an increase in fat consumption.

Neuropeptide Y, which is synthesized by neurons in the arcuate nucleus, stimulates food intake by activating the "feeding center" in the lateral hypothalamus. Ghrelin, a gut peptide secreted by endocrine cells in the stomach lining, stimulates arcuate neurons, with a resulting increase in food intake. Activation of leptin receptors in the arcuate nucleus inhibits the production of neuropeptide Y. Leptin is a peptide produced by fat cells (adipocytes), and its concentration in the blood is directly proportional to the amount of body fat. Arcuate neurons are also responsive to insulin, which inhibits food intake. Projections from the neurons that produce neuropeptide Y in the arcuate nucleus to the paraventricular nucleus produce increases in glucocorticoid secretion and insulin secretion, which lowers body temperature and causes a decrease in the breakdown of triglycerides (fatty acids). These energy-conserving metabolic changes probably result from activation of the pathway descending to the autonomic system from the paraventricular nucleus.

Located in the ventromedial nucleus of the hypothalamus is a satiety center. This area of the hypothalamus is activated when blood glucose levels rise after a meal. This helps us realize when we have had enough to eat and are no longer hungry. Damage to this area causes a person to eat too much (primarily carbohydrates) and eventually results in obesity.

THE HYPOTHALAMUS AND CIRCADIAN RHYTHMS

Many physiological functions fluctuate in a regular day-to-day cycle called a *circadian rhythm*. These rhythms are controlled by neurons in the SCN, which is sometimes referred to as the circadian pacemaker. Information about the light/dark cycle reaches the SCN through the retinohypothalamic tract, a direct projection from the retina containing axons from about 1% of the ganglion cells from all areas of the retina. Daily rhythms in the release of hormones from other hypothalamic nuclei are controlled by neural projections from the SCN. These hormones in turn influence daily activities such as eating, drinking, and sleeping. Daily fluctuations in the secretion of adrenal hormones are controlled by projections of the SCN to the paraventricular nucleus, which sends projections to sympathetic preganglionic neurons that synapse on the adrenal medulla. Secretion of melatonin is controlled by descending projections from the paraventricular nucleus to the sympathetic preganglionic neurons in the superior cervical ganglion, which projects to the pineal gland. The pineal gland, located on the surface of the midbrain just in front of the cerebellum, controls seasonal rhythms through its release of melatonin. In response to signals sent from the SCN through this indirect pathway, melatonin is secreted at night, with more being secreted on longer nights, such as during the winter. Activation by melatonin of its receptors on the SCN and other brain structures controls seasonal variations in physiological processes and secretion of hormones.

There is evidence that melatonin may also be involved in the synchronization of circadian rhythms.

THE HYPOTHALAMUS AND THE AUTONOMIC NERVOUS SYSTEM

In addition to its role in regulating the endocrine system, the hypothalamus also plays a key role in controlling the autonomic nervous system. Most of the hypothalamic neurons involved in the regulation of the autonomic nervous system are found in the paraventricular nucleus. There are three groups of neurons in the paraventricular nucleus. One group produces corticotropin-releasing hormone (CRH), a second group produces oxytocin and vasopressin, and a third group sends projections through a descending pathway to the brainstem and spinal cord.

Although the third group of neurons does not project to the posterior pituitary lobe, these neurons release the peptide neurotransmitters oxytocin and vasopressin, along with glutamate. Their axons descend in the median forebrain bundle, which they leave in the brainstem to synapse on parasympathetic nuclei there or continue in a lateral pathway to synapse on the parasympathetic and sympathetic preganglionic neurons in the spinal cord. Neurons in the lateral hypothalamus, the posterior hypothalamus, and the dorsomedial hypothalamic nucleus also send projections through the descending pathway as well as to brainstem nuclei. Some hypothalamic areas project through the dorsal longitudinal fasciculus, which descends more medially near the ventricular system.

HYPOTHALAMUS AND STRESS RESPONSE

Stressors are stimuli that the brain perceives as a threat to homeostasis (physiological balance and normal functioning). Physical stressors include extreme temperatures, trauma, hypoglycemia, severe hypotension, and exercise. Psychological stressors include situations that produce negative emotions, such as fear and anxiety, or that require intense mental effort.

Both types of stressors can trigger the **stress response**—a coordinated series of physiological reactions that prepares the body to cope with the perceived threat. Short-term activation of the stress response helps preserve homeostasis. However, long-term activation of the stress response can be destructive.

During the stress response, the noradrenergic system, the sympathetic nervous system (SNS), and the **hypothalamic-pituitary-adrenal (HPA) axis** become active. A projection from the central nucleus of the amygdala to the locus coeruleus is thought to activate the noradrenergic system. Activation of the SNS and the HPA axis involves the hypothalamus, which may also be influenced by amygdalar projections.

The paraventricular hypothalamic nucleus, which plays an important role in the stress response, is activated by inputs from the amygdala, lateral hypothalamus, locus coeruleus, prefrontal cortex, and hippocampus. A group of neurons in the paraventricular nucleus is responsible for activating the sympathetic nervous system, which then releases norepinephrine. Norepinephrine stimulates beta-adrenergic receptors in the cell membranes of the tissues and organs they innervate (including the heart and blood vessels). There are two exceptions to this general rule. Sympathetic postganglionic terminals connected to sweat glands release acetylcholine to bind with receptors on the postsynaptic membrane. The adrenal medulla (which is considered to be a sympathetic ganglion) is also activated by cholinergic nicotinic receptors rather than beta-adrenergic receptors. Secretory cells of the adrenal medulla then release norepinephrine and epinephrine into the bloodstream.

Activation of the sympathetic nervous system increases blood pressure and heart rate, dilates the pupils, shifts blood circulation to the brain and muscles, slows digestion, increases breathing rate, releases glucose from the liver and fatty acids from adipose (fatty) tissue, and decreases insulin production by the pancreas. Because all tissues except the brain tissue need insulin to use glucose, the reduced amount of insulin lets the brain have a larger share of the circulating glucose available. All of these physiological changes prepare the body for "fight or flight" to cope with threatening situations.

Another group of neurons in the paraventricular nucleus synthesizes CRH. This hormone triggers the activation of the HPA axis by stimulating the production and release of adrenocorticotropic-releasing hormone (ACTH) by the anterior pituitary. ACTH then travels through the bloodstream to the adrenal cortex, where it stimulates the production and release of cortisol. Like norepinephrine and epinephrine, cortisol mobilizes the body's energy stores.

NEUROENDOCRINE: IMMUNE INTERACTIONS

The autonomic nervous system, which links the brain to the immune system, innervates the bone marrow, thymus gland, spleen, and lymph nodes. Both parasympathetic and sympathetic fibers connect to these immune organs. Neurotransmitter receptors for norepinephrine, epinephrine, dopamine, acetylcholine, serotonin, opioids, and gamma-amino butyric acid (GABA) are found on leukocytes (white blood cells) and on lymphoid organs. Norepinephrine and epinephrine produced by the sympathetic nervous system during the stress response suppress the immune system. Acetylcholine, on the other hand, which is produced by the parasympathetic nervous system, stimulates the immune response. Opioids and dopamine are immunosuppressives, whereas GABA is an immunostimulant.

Neurons in many brain regions have cytokine receptors. *Cytokines*, or immunotransmitters, are chemical messengers secreted by white blood cells in response to inflammation or invasion by foreign organisms. Cytokines enter the brain through membrane transporters. Neurons, microglia, and astrocytes also produce cytokines. Increased levels of cytokines resulting from infection or inflammation can affect the release of neurotransmitters in the brain. When cytokines are used to treat cancers, neurodegenerative diseases, and infections, they can cause negative behavioral and neurological effects, such as memory problems, depression, paranoia, agitation, and impaired motor coordination.

Cytokines produced during inflammatory reactions can act on the hypothalamus as well as the pituitary gland to stimulate CRH release and ACTH release, thereby activating the HPA axis. Although physiological levels of cortisol are

WHAT IS AUTOIMMUNE DISEASE?

Autoimmune disease results when the body produces antibodies or immune cells that attack the body's own cells. These self-attacking antibodies and immune cells, also called *autoantibodies* and *autoreactive T lymphocytes,* respectively, cause damage to body tissues. A healthy immune system has the capacity to produce antibodies and T lymphocytes (also called T cells) that react to "self" instead of "foreign" proteins, a capacity that may be essential for normal functioning. However, with autoimmune disease, the inhibitory processes that prevent the immune system from producing too many of these autoreactive antibodies and cells are somehow disrupted. Development of autoimmune disease can be triggered by viral infections, certain drugs, hormones, environmental factors, and even sunlight, as in the case of systemic lupus erythematosus. The chemical element mercury, which is found in dental fillings and vaccine preparations, has also been implicated. More than 80 autoimmune diseases affect over 10 million Americans, 75% of whom are female. In most autoimmune diseases, a protein specific to a certain organ or tissue is targeted, but in some, such as systemic lupus erythematosus, the protein targeted is widespread enough that an inflammatory response takes place throughout the entire body. Autoimmune diseases of the nervous system include multiple sclerosis and myasthenia gravis. Scientists have found evidence that autoimmune processes may cause other dysfunctions of the nervous system, including obsessive-compulsive disorder, schizophrenia, and Alzheimer's disease. It is becoming apparent that having a healthy immune system is essential to having a healthy nervous system.

necessary for normal development and optimal functioning of the immune system, the levels of cortisol present during the stress response primarily suppress the immune response. Cytokines not only increase glucocorticoid production but also modify the sensitivity of immune cells to cortisol. Activation of glucocorticoid receptors on leucocytes by cortisol may be part of a feedback response to prevent the inflammatory response from spinning out of control. However, if elevated levels of cortisol are sustained over long periods of time, illness can result due to lowered resistance to infections and tumor formation.

CONNECTIONS

Through its control of pituitary gland secretion and the autonomic nervous system, the tiny hypothalamus has far-reaching effects on maintaining the homeostasis of body functions and on the body's reaction to stress. The hypothalamus and the secretion of the hormones it controls also regulate eating, drinking, and reproductive behavior. Circadian rhythms, or daily patterns of fluctuation in body rhythms, including the sleep/wake cycle, are under the control of the hypothalamus. Innervation of immune organs by the autonomic nervous system and the presence of receptors for neurotransmitters on immune cells and organs show the interaction between the immune system and the nervous system. Because nerve cells have receptors for cytokines, or immunotransmitters, it is apparent that this is a two-way interaction. Not only does the nervous system regulate the functions of the immune system, but the immune system, through its own set of chemical messengers, affects brain functions, including mood and cognition. Cytokines produced during inflammatory responses act on the hypothalamus to activate the HPA axis and thus control the immune response. This represents an interaction between the neuroimmune system and the endocrine system.

9

Sleep and Wakefulness

You may not think about it often, but sleep is a very important part of your life. Most people spend one-third of their entire lives sleeping! Many people think that the brain is inactive during sleep, but they're mistaken. In fact, sleep is an active, highly regulated process. Although we have less awareness of and fewer responses to environmental stimuli while we sleep, most of the brain's activities do not change. Some studies suggest that the 90-minute cycles that occur during sleep may be part of an overall rest-activity cycle that occurs in 90-minute cycles throughout the 24-hour day. This phenomenon was named the **basic rest-activity cycle (BRAC)** by American scientist Nathaniel Kleitman (1895–1999), who set up the first sleep research laboratory and is considered the "father of sleep research." Other studies have emphasized the role of a **circadian pacemaker** in the regulation of the sleep/wake cycle and its synchronization with the light/dark pattern over a 24-hour period.

Although scientists have made great progress in understanding sleep over the last few decades, the reasons we sleep are not yet completely understood. At one time, experts believed that the only purpose of sleep was to give the body physical rest and restoration. Studies of the biochemical changes that occur during sleep, however, suggest that this is not the case. Scientists found that a person's level of physical activity during the day does not correlate with the amount of deep sleep he or she gets that night. The amount of mental activity during the day, however, *does* relate to the amount of deep sleep we get at night. Currently, there is a growing consensus that the reason we sleep is to rest and restore the brain.

AROUSAL AND WAKEFULNESS

A fiber system called the **ascending reticular activating system (ARAS)** helps control arousal and wakefulness (Figure 9.1). The ARAS ascends from cholinergic, adrenergic, dopaminergic, and serotonergic nuclei in the brainstem. In addition to these brainstem nuclei, there are wake-promoting areas in both the forebrain and the hypothalamus. Cholinergic neurons in the basal forebrain project directly to the cortex and promote wakefulness and arousal. Histaminergic neurons in the posterior hypothalamus project diffusely to the cerebral cortex and promote wakefulness. Orexin hypocretin-producing neurons located in the lateral hypothalamus project widely in the brain and to the spinal cord. Orexins, which also influence eating behavior, seem to be important in keeping us alert. A deficiency in orexin transmission, possibly due to an autoimmune reaction that deactivates or destroys orexin receptors, has been suggested as one of the causes of **narcolepsy**, a disorder in which a person is constantly sleepy during the daytime. Continuous activity of all of these wake-promoting neurons is necessary to maintain wakefulness.

When we are awake, cholinergic and other ARAS inputs to the thalamic relay nuclei enhance thalamic transmission, which keeps the cerebral cortex continuously active. As you will recall, fibers carrying sensory information from all the senses except smell travel to the thalamus, which relays their messages to the cerebral cortex. Collaterals, or branches, of these fibers also end in the reticular formation. When the ARAS is inhibited,

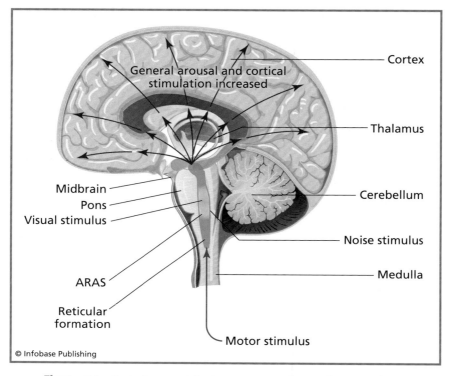

Figure 9.1 Brainstem nuclei whose axons make up the ascending reticular activating system (ARAS) include the locus coeruleus (norepinephrine), the raphe nuclei (serotonin), the ventral tegmental area (dopamine), and the pediculopontine tegmental (PPT) and laterodorsal tegmental (LDT) nuclei (acetylcholine). The ARAS causes activation, or arousal, of the cerebral cortex both by direct projections to the cortex and indirectly through relays in the thalamus, posterior hypothalamus, and septal nuclei.

transmission of sensory information through the thalamus is also inhibited. This produces the reduction in awareness that is typical of sleep.

SLEEP

Sleep is promoted by signals from the anterior hypothalamus. When the anterior hypothalamus is electrically stimulated, it induces sleep. The pupils of the eye constrict and there is a decrease in heart rate, blood pressure, and body temperature. A group of GABAergic neurons in the hypothalamic ventrolateral preoptic nucleus (VLPO) project to the serotonergic and noradrenergic nuclei in the brainstem and promote sleep by inhibiting their activity. Galanin, which is released along with gamma-amino butyric acid (GABA) from these neurons, also promotes sleep. GABAergic fibers from the VLPO nucleus also terminate in the posterior hypothalamus. The histaminergic nuclei are most active during wakefulness, less active during NREM (non-rapid eye movement) sleep, and inactive during REM (rapid eye movement) sleep. Neurons in the hypothalamic

NATHANIEL KLEITMAN: THE FATHER OF SLEEP RESEARCH

Nathaniel Kleitman, popularly known as the father of sleep research, set up the first sleep lab soon after he joined the faculty at the University of Chicago in 1925. His first major book on sleep, called *Sleep and Wakefulness*, was published in 1939. It is still an important work in sleep research.

Kleitman used volunteers from the university for some of his experiments, but his main subjects were often members of his own family. From the time they were infants, Kleitman meticulously studied the sleeping habits of his two daughters. Once, Kleitman himself deliberately stayed awake for 180 hours to study the effects of sleep deprivation.

Kleitman is particularly noted for his important discoveries. Along with some of the students who helped him, Kleitman was the first to report the existence of **REM** (rapid eye movement) **sleep**, and was the first to measure eye movement and use **electroencephalograms (EEGs)** to chart the stages of sleep.

Kleitman was born in Russia in 1895 and became an American citizen in 1918. He had a long career and a long life—he died in 1999 at the age of 104.

medial preoptic nucleus, some of which secrete serotonin and adenosine, also promote sleep. The medial preoptic nucleus has connections to many brain areas and is close to the suprachiasmatic nucleus (SCN) and the areas that regulate temperature. It acts on the parasympathetic nervous system to lower blood pressure, slow heart rate, and constrict the pupils during NREM sleep.

Sleepiness appears to be regulated by homeostatic and circadian mechanisms. How long and how deeply we sleep after we have experienced a sleep loss is proportional to the length of time we were awake—that is, sleep varies with the duration of prior wakefulness. Sleepiness also appears to vary in a circadian cycle. Increases in sleepiness in the evening and at approximately 3 P.M. to 4 P.M. coincide with the lowest levels of cortisol during its circadian cycle.

TYPES OF SLEEP

There are two basic types of sleep: **synchronized**, or **nonREM sleep**, and **desynchronized**, or REM sleep, which is named after the characteristic eye movements that occur during this type of sleep. About every 90 minutes, the sleep cycle shifts from nonREM sleep to REM sleep. Ranging from 5 to 30 minutes, periods of REM sleep get longer each time the body reaches the REM stage during the night (Figure 9.2).

Brain activity during sleep can be monitored by attaching electrodes to a person's scalp. The brain waves that the electrodes detect are recorded as an EEG. Electrodes attached near the eyes monitor eye movements and record the results as an **electro-oculogram (EOG)**. Muscle activity is monitored with electrodes attached to the chin and recorded as an **electromyogram (EMG)**.

There are two main types of electrical activity in the brain during wakefulness: **alpha rhythms** and **beta rhythms**. Alpha rhythms occur during quiet rest, usually with closed eyes. During alpha activity, regular waves occur at a frequency of 8 to 12 cycles per second. Beta rhythms, on the other hand, occur

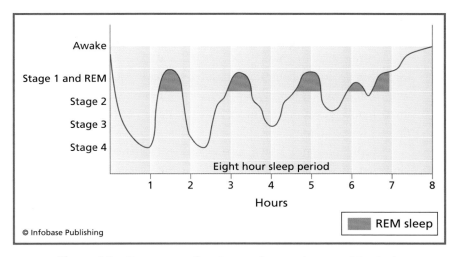

Figure 9.2   On average, the sleep cycle repeats every 90 minutes, resulting in 4 or 5 cycles during the night. As the night progresses, the time spent in Stages 3 and 4 decreases. In fact, most deep sleep occurs during the first half of the night. During the rest of the night, Stage 2 sleep and REM sleep increase more during each sleep cycle. Meaningful stimuli (like someone saying your name) will awaken you during REM sleep, but only loud noises will awaken you from Stage 4 sleep. You will be groggy and confused if awakened from deep sleep but alert and attentive if awakened during REM sleep.

during periods of alertness, attentiveness, or active thought. Beta waves are irregular in size and of low amplitude and occur at a frequency of 13 to 30 cycles per second. The more active the brain is, the lower the amplitude and the higher the frequency (number per second) of the brain waves shown by the EEG.

STAGES OF SLEEP

There are four stages of NREM sleep. As drowsiness sets in, we transition from wakefulness to sleep. This sleep stage is characterized by alpha activity and some theta activity, which has a frequency of 3.5–7.5 cycles per second. In Stage 1, we drift in and out of sleep—although the actual changeover from wakefulness to sleep happens instantaneously, not gradually. During this stage, muscles start to relax and breathing gets slower.

We are still conscious enough, however, to become quickly alert if we hear a noise or are disturbed in some other way.

During Stage 2 of NREM sleep, the brain waves are irregular. While in Stage 2 sleep, a person's eyes move slowly from side to side. Although the sleeper can still be roused fairly easily, it would take a much louder noise to wake a person from Stage 2 sleep than it would from Stage 1.

Stages 3 and 4 are known as **slow-wave sleep**, or **deep sleep**. A person in Stage 3 sleep is transitioning into deep sleep and becoming progressively more difficult to arouse. People who are awakened during deep sleep usually do not report dreaming, but if they do, the dreams are usually nightmares.

Blood pressure, heart rate, systemic vascular resistance, and cardiac output remain regular but decline as we move to later stages of NREM sleep. Parasympathetic activity increases, whereas sympathetic activity decreases. Because the heart does not have to work as hard, it can replenish its cardiac metabolic stores. This replenishment is necessary to keep the heart muscle healthy.

During sleep, we no longer have voluntary control over our breathing. Periodic breathing, with a repeating pattern of increases and decreases in breathing amplitude, occurs during Stage 1 and sometimes into Stage 2 sleep. Stages 3 and 4 are characterized by regular breathing frequency and amplitude. Thermoregulatory responses (activities that regulate body temperature), such as sweating and shivering, remain active.

REM SLEEP

About 90 minutes after the onset of Stage 1 sleep, the EEG changes suddenly to resemble the irregular pattern of the waking EEG. REM sleep is called "paradoxical sleep" because the electrical activity of the brain resembles that of the waking or Stage 1 EEG. People awakened from REM sleep report vivid, storylike dreams. REM sleep is named after the rapid eye movements that are characteristic of this type of sleep.

A loss of muscle tone is present during REM sleep and is caused by the inhibition of motor neurons in the spinal cord by glycinergic interneurons. This loss of muscle tone prevents us from acting out our dreams and possibly hurting ourselves.

During REM sleep, sympathetic tone is increased, and peripheral blood flow is reduced except to the heart and skeletal muscles. Heart rate varies a lot; it may have very slow or very fast episodes. Breathing is irregular and activity of the diaphragm increases. The metabolic rate either increases or shows no change. Cerebral blood flow and general metabolism are both near waking levels.

CIRCADIAN INFLUENCES ON SLEEP

Whether we sleep or wake depends on the interplay of several neurotransmitter systems in the brain, as well as the influences of hypothalamic nuclei (Figure 9.3). Sleep/wake cycle timing is regulated by the SCN. Firing rates of suprachiasmatic neurons are low at night and high during the day. There are projections from the SCN to the thalamus, the basal forebrain, and the subventricular and dorsal zones of the hypothalamus. Direct projections to the hypocretin/orexin neurons may be involved in the SCN's promotion of wakefulness.

Melatonin secretion, which is low during the light phase and high during the dark phase, is also regulated by the SCN. Projections from the SCN terminate in the hypothalamic subventricular zone, from which neurons project to preganglionic autonomic neurons in the spinal cord. **Postganglionic fibers** from the superior cervical ganglion in the neck project to the pineal gland, which secretes melatonin. Although the pineal gland appears to be the primary source of circulating melatonin, melatonin is also synthesized in the gastrointestinal tract and the retina, as well as a number of other places. It circulates in the cerebrospinal fluid and in the blood and reaches all areas of the brain and body. Under the control of the SCN, it acts as an indirect circadian messenger and helps to synchronize

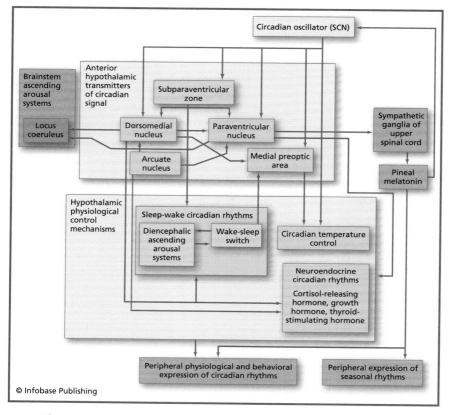

Figure 9.3 This flow chart depicts the interactions of the suprachiasmatic nucleus (SCN) directly and indirectly with other hypothalamic nuclei and indirectly with the pineal gland in the circadian control of the sleep/wake cycle and physiological functions. Feedback from the pineal gland, which produces melatonin, is also shown. This feedback is thought to have a modulatory influence on the SCN's control of circadian rhythms.

sleep with the day/night cycle. Once secreted, melatonin has an inhibitory feedback effect on the mechanisms of the SCN that promote wakefulness.

Plasma concentrations of melatonin start to rise between 9 P.M. and 10 P.M., peak between 2 A.M. and 4 A.M., and then decline until the low daytime levels are reached between 7 A.M. and 9 A.M. Exposure to light can cause a phase change in melatonin secretion. Prolonged exposure to light during the evening hours delays the secretion of melatonin, and prolonged exposure to darkness during the morning hours extends melatonin secretion. Brief light exposures during the night will temporarily decrease melatonin secretion. Melatonin levels range from very low in infants to maximum levels in children around age 3. This is followed by a decline, which is pronounced during puberty. The decline in melatonin levels is complete by age 20 to 30, after which the levels remain stable. There is a 20-fold variation between individuals in the amount of melatonin they secrete.

Melatonin is an immune enhancer, a vasoconstrictor, and a mild anticonvulsant. It reduces luteinizing hormone (LH) and prolactin secretion and delays puberty until its levels start to decline. Taking vitamin B_6 or tryptophan causes the brain to produce more melatonin. When people who have insomnia take melatonin, they often get some relief. However, due to melatonin's vasoconstrictive actions, caution should be used for those who have high blood pressure.

SLEEP AND MEMORY

Scientists continue to debate whether sleep does indeed play a role in memory consolidation and, if so, which stages of sleep are most important. A lot has yet to be learned about the precise mechanisms by which sleep enhances certain types of memory during the different stages of sleep. But scientists are using a variety of techniques, including neuroimaging techniques, recording patterns of brain waves during sleep after a learning task, studying the effects of drugs and hormones on consolidation, and comparing the effects of different patterns of sleep on retention of learning tasks.

As a result of these studies, there is growing evidence that sleep during the first half of the night, when slow-wave sleep (SWS) predominates, enhances the storage of declarative memories, including episodic memory and semantic memory. Likewise, during the second half of the night, when REM sleep predominates, sleep appears to enhance the consolidation of emotional memories and procedural memories, including those involving motor skills.

There also appears to be an interaction between cortisol levels and the stage of sleep in their effects on memory consolidation. Cortisol levels are at their lowest during the first half of the night and grow progressively higher during the second half of the night. Increasing cortisol levels during early sleep or decreasing it during late sleep interferes with the consolidation of declarative memories. Consolidation of procedural memories, which are hippocampal independent, is not affected. Decreasing cortisol during late sleep also enhances the storage of emotional memories, which may be held in check by the normally high cortisol levels.

SLEEP-RELATED PROBLEMS

Insomnia, the most common sleep complaint, is actually a symptom rather than a disorder. Although most people experience insomnia at some point in their lives, it can also be a component of such conditions as Alzheimer's disease or African sleeping sickness. According to surveys, 10 to 15% of adults in the developed world have insomnia at any given time, and one-third of the population experiences insomnia to some degree each year.

Excessive daytime sleepiness, which occurs in about 5% of adults, is also a symptom as opposed to a disorder. It is most common in shift workers (people who work at night or in rotating shifts), young adults, and the elderly, and it is associated with snoring, sleep deprivation, and the use of hypnotic (sleep-inducing) drugs.

There are several types of sleepiness. Subalertness is a reduced arousal state that varies with the circadian rhythm phase and the quality and duration of the last period of sleep. Drowsiness is sleepiness during the day that does not necessarily result in sleep. Microsleeps are sleep episodes that occur during the day and last only a few seconds.

Narcolepsy is a disorder in which REM sleep occurs during waking hours. There is some evidence that it happens because of a deficiency in orexin/hypocretin, possibly due to a genetic mutation or an autoimmune reaction. Brain damage occasionally causes narcolepsy. The sleep attack is the primary symptom of narcolepsy. A sleep attack is an overwhelming need to sleep that usually occurs when conditions are monotonous. It results in 2 to 5 minutes of REM sleep and leaves the person feeling refreshed. In cataplexy (another symptom of narcolepsy), sleep atonia—or sleep paralysis, a component of REM sleep—occurs suddenly. The person falls to the ground and lies there for several seconds up to several minutes without losing awareness. Cataplexy usually results from a sudden physical movement in response to an unexpected event or to strong emotions such as anger or laughter.

SLEEPWALKING

Somnambulism, or sleepwalking, is a state of incomplete arousal during Stage 3 or 4 of slow-wave sleep. It is most common in young adults and children and may even be seen in infancy—the child will crawl around while sleeping. Onset of sleepwalking usually occurs after the age of 18 months. It is most prevalent between ages 11 and 12; some 16.7% of people this age sleepwalk. More males than females are sleepwalkers. Sleepwalking that begins before age 9 may continue into adulthood. Episodes may range in frequency from less than once a month to almost every night in severe cases. Fever, noise in the sleep environment, stress, a distended bladder, and pain can bring on an episode. Most cases of sleepwalking do not result in physical harm, but there have been cases of physical injury and a few cases of violent behavior. Preventive measures for vulnerable individuals include getting adequate rest, relaxing before going to bed, using a ground-floor bedroom, placing furniture in front of large windows, and ensuring that doors and windows are not easy to open.

Hypnagogic hallucinations occur when REM dreaming accompanies sleep paralysis while the person is awake just before or after sleep. REM sleep behavior disorder is a condition in which normal sleep paralysis does not occur and the person acts out the vivid dreams he or she has during REM sleep. It is most common during the first round of REM sleep of the night. Like narcolepsy, it appears to have a genetic component and can also result from brain damage. The movements made can range from twitches to arm flailing, talking, running, jumping, or aggressive acts. It is most common after age 50 and is four times more common in males than in females.

CONNECTIONS

Sleep is an active process, as scientists have demonstrated by observing electrical activity on an EEG during the various stages of sleep. In the 90-minute sleep cycle, four progressively deepening stages of NREM sleep come before an episode of REM sleep. Also known as paradoxical sleep because the brain's electrical activity is so similar to that of the waking state, REM sleep is characterized by vivid dreams and a loss of muscle tone. Wakefulness is promoted by serotonergic and noradrenergic nuclei in the brainstem and by histaminergic neurons in the posterior hypothalamus. GABAergic neurons in the VLPO nucleus in the anterior hypothalamus promote sleep by inhibiting these neurons. Cholinergic neurons in the basal forebrain promote wakefulness, and nuclei in the pons promote REM sleep. This latter set of cholinergic neurons is inhibited by serotinergic and noradrenergic projections, which become silent during REM sleep. Orexin neurons in the lateral hypothalamus promote wakefulness by projecting to cholinergic, histaminergic, and monoaminergic neurons.

Timing of the sleep/wake cycle is regulated by the SCN of the thalamus. Melatonin helps synchronize the sleep/wake cycle with the day/night cycle. Sleep deprivation results in suppression of immune functions. Infections promote sleep as do increased levels of cytokines in the absence of infection. A number of neurochemicals, including adenosine, serotonin metabolites, cholecystokinin, and neuropeptide Y have been identified as potential candidates for endogenous sleep-inducing substances.

The production of growth hormone, prolactin, thyroid-stimulating hormone (TSH), and cortisol are all regulated by the sleep/wake cycle. The secretion of growth hormone and prolactin are primarily controlled by the sleep/wake cycle, whereas cortisol secretion is somewhat influenced by sleep but is primarily under circadian control, and thyrotropin secretion has a circadian rhythm but is inhibited by sleep.

10

Diseases and Injuries of the Nervous System

Few of us will go through life without being affected, either personally or through a friend or relative, by some kind of disease or injury of the nervous system. What effect a nervous system disease or injury has depends greatly on where in the nervous system it occurs. For example, damage to a group of neurons in the brain may have far-reaching effects, whereas damage to a peripheral nerve will have more localized effects. Likewise, bilateral damage to brain and spinal cord areas produces much greater impairment of function than does unilateral damage. Some effects of injuries and disorders are so subtle that they are almost unnoticeable. Others can be devastating to a person's daily life.

DISEASE AND INJURIES OF THE NEUROMUSCULAR SYSTEM

Diseases and disorders that affect the neuromuscular system can impair movement. Such conditions can be caused by viruses, environmental toxins, autoimmune responses, and side effects of medications. Some conditions involve genetic factors, meaning that they result from a specific gene mutation or from a genetic predisposition or susceptibility. The effects of these diseases can be crippling and even lethal.

NEUROMUSCULAR AUTOIMMUNE DISEASES

Autoimmune diseases occur when the immune system attacks the body's own proteins as if they were foreign proteins. Myasthenia gravis is an autoimmune disorder in which antibodies form against the nicotinic receptors at the neuromuscular junction. These antibodies block the receptors and cause muscle weakness. Symptoms include drooping eyelids, double vision, problems swallowing and talking, and general weakness and fatigue. This disorder affects 3 to 4 people out of 100,000 and is usually progressive, ultimately ending in death.

Multiple sclerosis (MS) is an autoimmune disease in which antibodies to myelin break down the myelin sheath that surrounds the axons of neurons of the brain and spinal cord. This destruction of myelin causes nerve impulses to move more slowly through the nerve fibers. Symptoms of MS can include visual problems, fatigue, pain, numbness, tingling, problems with walking, depression, bowel or bladder problems, sexual dysfunction, and problems with attention, memory, and problem-solving. Less common symptoms include tremor, speech problems, impaired hearing, difficulty swallowing, and a lack of coordination. Several viruses (including those that cause German measles, mononucleosis, and canine distemper) have been implicated as possible causes of MS, either by destroying the myelin sheath or by triggering an autoimmune response. The connection of these viruses to MS, however, has not yet been proven. Genetic factors that make a person more susceptible to an environmental factor that could trigger the disease may also play a role. MS can be mild, moderate, or severe—the course and symptoms vary a great deal from person to person. Despite the potential seriousness of the disease, most people with MS now live out 95% of their normal lifespan.

BASAL GANGLIA DISORDERS

Parkinson's disease is a movement disorder caused by the degeneration of neurons in the substantia nigra that produce dopamine (Figure 10.1). Parkinson's disease usually appears in people between the ages of 50 and 60. Analysis of brain tissue from Parkinson's patients who have died has shown a loss of the black pigment that is normally seen in the substantia nigra. This pigment is called *neuromelanin* and is a by-product of dopamine metabolism. Symptoms of Parkinson's disease include problems with initiating movements, slowness in movement, rigidity due to increased muscle tone, and tremors of the hands, arms, and head when they are at rest. Problems with posture, equilibrium, and the function of the autonomic nervous system may also be present. Speech is slow and monotonous, handwriting becomes very small, and facial expressions are lost.

Although the etiology (causes) of most Parkinson's cases is not understood yet, toxic agents may cause damage to the substantia nigra and produce symptoms of the disease. Postencephalitic Parkinsonism occurred in some people who survived an epidemic between 1919 and 1929 of encephalitis lethargica. Carbon monoxide and manganese poisoning can result in basal ganglia damage and Parkinsonian symptoms. Designer drugs, such as MPTP, can produce Parkinson's disease. Drug-induced Parkinson's disease occurs in 50% of patients who use neuroleptic (antipsychotic) drugs over a long period of time.

Degeneration of neurons (particularly those that produce acetylcholine and gamma-amino butyric acid [GABA]) of the putamen and the caudate nucleus results in a disorder called Huntington's chorea. Wasting (atrophy) of the tissue of the cerebral cortex also occurs. Symptoms, which include involuntary movements (particularly of the limbs), usually appear when the victim is between age 35 and 45, but may appear as

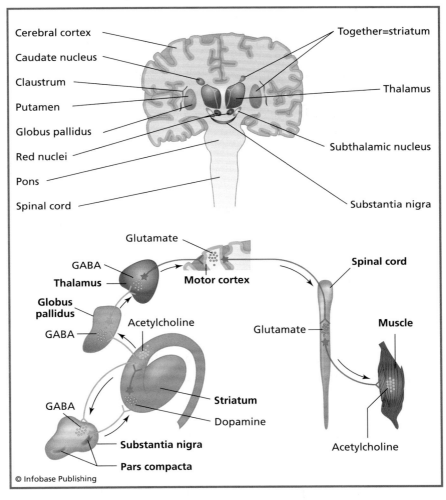

Figure 10.1 Except for the claustrum, whose function is unknown, the structures (or portions thereof) shown in the upper figure play a part in the control of movement. The lower figure shows how the basal ganglia interact to help control movement indirectly through their effect on the thalamus. In Parkinson's disease, up to 80% of the dopaminergic neurons in the substantia nigra are destroyed. Cholinergic interneurons in the striatum, which are normally inhibited by dopamine, become overactive. Cholinergic overactivity in the striatum is considered the primary cause of the rigidity and tremors of Parkinson's disease.

early as the twenties and sometimes even during childhood. Progressive dementia and emotional problems, including depression, can be part of this disorder. The disease, which has been traced to a mutation of a dominant gene located on chromosome 4, is hereditary, and it always ends in death. Children of parents who have Huntington's chorea have a 50% chance of inheriting this gene.

Hemiballismus is a movement disorder caused by damage to one of the pair of subthalamic nuclei, usually as the result of a stroke. Symptoms include flailing movements of the limb or extremity on the contralateral side of the body. This condition may spontaneously resolve after a period of several weeks.

Prolonged use of antipsychotic drugs produces a largely irreversible movement disorder called tardive dyskinesia in 50% or more of patients. Symptoms of this disorder include facial tics, grimacing, rapid eye blinking, peculiar gestures, cheek puffing, tongue protrusion, and lip pursing. Writhing movements of the trunk and hands are sometimes present as well. Because the basal ganglia, which are impaired in this disorder, play a role in higher cognitive functions, many tardive dyskinesia patients also develop **dementia**. Scientists theorize that the disorder is caused by a compensatory increase of dopaminergic receptors in the postsynaptic membrane in response to the inhibition of dopaminergic receptors by antipsychotic drugs, which are dopamine antagonists.

CEREBELLAR DISORDERS

Damage to the cerebellum results in loss of coordination and reduced muscle tone. The specific symptoms depend on which area of the cerebellum is damaged. One common symptom is **ataxia**, or "drunken gait." Goose-stepping, or high stepping, may occur. **Movement decomposition**, in which smooth motions decompose into a jerky series of discrete movements, may be present. Another symptom of cerebellar damage is dysmetria, an overshooting of targets—for example, when the person points. **Intention tremor**, or tremor while a limb or extremity is in motion (as opposed to the resting tremor seen in Parkinson's), may occur. An inability to produce rapid alternating movements, such as fingertapping, may be present. Unilateral damage to the cerebellum affects only the ipsilateral (same) side, so symptoms are seen in the extremities only on that side.

MOTOR NEURON DISEASE

Amyotrophic lateral sclerosis (ALS), also known as *Lou Gehrig's disease*, results when the motor neurons in the brain, brainstem, and spinal cord degenerate and the lateral corticospinal tracts deteriorate. Symptoms include hyperactive reflexes, atrophy of muscles, muscle weakness, and fasciculations, or spasms of the fibers of a single motor unit. Survival with this disease is usually from 3 to 5 years.

Apraxias are problems performing learned skilled movements due to damage to the frontal or parietal lobes or to the corpus callosum. They can involve difficulties in performing tasks with the fingers, hands, or arms; speech impairments due to movement problems with speech muscles; and problems with constructing, assembling, or drawing objects.

EPILEPSY

Epilepsy is a neurological condition in which recurring seizures are the main symptom. It affects about 0.4 to 0.8% of the population. A seizure occurs when a large group of neurons fires together repetitively in synchrony. Everyone's brain is able to produce a seizure under certain conditions. Some people may have lower thresholds for seizure activity and may therefore be more susceptible to having spontaneous seizures. Seizures can be triggered in vulnerable individuals by emotional stress, sleep deprivation, alcohol withdrawal, menstrual cycle phases, and sometimes specific stimuli such as strobe lights. Seizures may also be caused by reduced levels of certain neurotransmitters (Figure 10.2). Seizure thresholds may be lowered in areas of the brain that have suffered damage from trauma, stroke, brain infection (such as meningitis or encephalitis), tumor, or neurodegenerative diseases.

Generalized epilepsy is a type of epilepsy in which large areas of both cerebral hemispheres seem to discharge at the same time. Most cases of generalized epilepsy begin before age 20. Generalized seizures include tonic-clonic, absence, atonic, and myoclonic seizures. Tonic-clonic seizures, or grand mal seizures, which are the most common type of generalized seizure, involve a loss of consciousness and a *tonic* phase (in which contraction of the muscles causes the body to stiffen), followed by a *clonic* phase (in which the muscles jerk uncontrollably). An absence seizure, or petit mal seizure, involves a transient loss of awareness that lasts only a few seconds and may be accompanied by a blank stare. Atonic seizures are also called **drop attacks** because the muscles lose their tone suddenly and the person falls to the floor. Myoclonic seizures involve a brief series of jerks.

Focal epilepsy, which may begin at any age, is a type of epilepsy in which the electrical discharge that causes the seizure begins in one particular area in the brain—usually a place where an injury (from trauma, stroke, tumor, prenatal toxin exposure, or other cause) has previously occurred. The abnormal electrical discharge can remain fixed at its point of origin, or *locus*, or it can spread to the rest of the brain to become a generalized seizure. The symptoms present at the beginning of a focal seizure may give a clue as to where its locus is located.

Focal seizures, also called partial seizures, include simple partial seizures and complex partial seizures. Simple partial seizures do not cause a loss of consciousness, and the symptoms may be a corruption of the functions of the area in which the locus of the seizure activity is found. Symptoms, which go away after several seconds, may include numbness, twitching, dizziness, nausea, sweating, or disturbances of vision, hearing, taste, or smell. Complex partial seizures do involve a loss

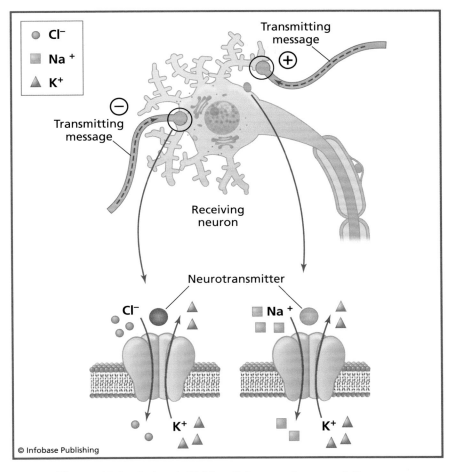

Figure 10.2   Reduced GABA activity may be one of the causes of some cases of epilepsy. Activation of the GABA receptor results in an influx of chloride (Cl⁻) ions into the cell. This results in a hyperpolarization of the cell and a decrease in the probability of an action potential. (The influx of sodium [Na⁺] ions has the opposite effect—it causes depolarization.) Under normal conditions, inhibitory GABAergic neurons keep excitatory glutamatergic neurons in check so that the brain is not overstimulated. In some epileptic brains, there may be reduced GABAergic transmission that may be due to lower levels of GABA, excessive deactivation of GABA by enzymes, or changes in the binding properties of GABA receptors. However, this is just one of the possible causes of epilepsy.

of awareness, and symptoms are not remembered afterwards. Strange behaviors such as lip smacking, repeated swallowing, plucking at clothing, or wandering around as if inebriated as well as symptoms similar to those of a simple partial seizure may occur.

SPINAL CORD INJURY

Approximately 11,000 cases of spinal cord injury (SCI) occur in the United States each year. There are a total of about 250,000 Americans living with SCIs today. The yearly figure does not include SCIs incurred in fatal accidents. A little over half (56%) of SCIs occur in young adults, with 31 years being the average age at the time of injury. Most SCIs (82%) occur in males. The primary causes of SCI are automobile accidents (37%), violence (28%), falls (21%), and sports (6%). SCI can also result from diseases of the spinal cord or vertebral column.

If the spinal column is fractured or displaced, it pinches the spinal cord and may cause contusion (bruising), along with edema (swelling) and hemorrhage (bleeding). An SCI may affect neurons within the spinal cord as well as the ascending and descending fiber pathways that travel through it. The **level of injury** is the lowest (bottommost) vertebral segment at which there is a decrease or absence of sensation and movement on both sides of the body. In **tetraplegia,** or **quadriplegia,** sensation and movement in all four limbs is lost due to an injury in the neck region. **Paraplegia** is the term used to describe injuries in the rest of the spinal cord. Depending on the level of injury, movement and sensation may be impaired anywhere from the middle of the chest downward through the lower extremities. Approximately 47% of SCIs result in tetraplegia, and about 52% result in paraplegia.

Extensive damage to the spinal cord can result in a complete SCI in which all sensation and movement is lost below the level of the injury. Complete SCIs make up nearly half of all SCIs. How much movement and sensation is preserved in an incomplete SCI depends on where the injury is and which nerve pathways run through the damaged area. Most SCI patients experience a loss of bladder and bowel control as well as sexual dysfunction. Chronic pain may be a problem, even in the areas of the body where other sensation is lost. The person may also lose the ability to sweat below the level of injury, which leads to problems with temperature control.

There is usually little recovery of function after a complete SCI. With an incomplete SCI, some recovery of function, which varies with the location of the injury, is usually seen. Any improvement that takes place usually begins within the first few days to the first 6 months after the injury. Most recovery of function occurs within the first year after the injury. Loss of function that remains after 1 to 2 years is usually permanent. There are exceptions to this general rule, however, including deceased actor Christopher Reeve, whose efforts to find effective treatments for himself and others stimulated research efforts that hold the promise of improved outcomes for SCI victims.

STROKE

Over 700,000 incidents of stroke occur each year in the United States, causing over 200,000 deaths. This makes stroke the third leading cause of death after heart disease and cancer. Risk factors for stroke include age, high blood pressure, cardiac disease, diabetes mellitus, smoking, high cholesterol, excessive use of alcohol, atherosclerosis of arteries in the neck and limbs, previous transient "ministrokes," oral contraceptive use, obesity, and lack of exercise.

The two basic types of stroke are *ischemic* (88% of all strokes) and *hemorrhagic* (12% of all strokes). Ischemia is the interruption of the blood supply to an area. In an ischemic stroke, an area of the brain is deprived of oxygen and glucose due to an interruption in blood supply. This type of stroke can be caused by **embolism**, thrombosis, or decreased systemic perfusion. Embolytic stroke is the most common form of ischemic

stroke. An embolism occurs when a blood clot formed somewhere else in the body blocks a blood vessel in the brain. Most
such clots form during heart attacks or atrial fibrillation, or
as a result of a dysfunction of the heart valves. Thrombosis
occurs when a blood vessel narrows due to disease processes or
is blocked by a blood clot or piece of atherosclerotic plaque or
other debris that breaks free from diseased blood vessel walls.
Decreased systemic perfusion can occur during heart attack or
arrhythmia (irregular heartbeat) or as the result of hypotension
(lowered blood pressure). Transient ischemic attacks (TIAs)
occur when the blockage of an artery is temporary, and the
thrombus or embolus is dislodged.

In a hemorrhagic stroke, blood is released onto the surface
of the brain, into the subarachnoid space, or into brain tissue.
Subarachnoid hemorrhage occurs when one of the large arteries at the base of the brain ruptures and fills the subarachnoid
space. This produces an increase in intracranial pressure that
can result in unconsciousness or death. Trauma is the most
common cause of subarachnoid hemorrhage. An aneurysm
is the ballooning of a weakened area in the wall of a blood
vessel. Rupture of an aneurysm is the major nontraumatic
cause of hemorrhagic stroke. Intracerebral hemorrhage, most
commonly caused by hypertension, results from the rupture
of small arteries within the brain. This allows blood to leak
into the brain tissue. Intracranial pressure is increased, and the
brain tissue swells.

Symptoms of stroke depend on the location and sever-
ity of the lesion. A lesion in the front left cerebral hemisphere causes symptoms that can include weakness and loss
of sensation in the right limb, aphasia, problems with the
right visual field, and difficulties with writing, reading, and
making calculations. If the lesion is in the front right hemisphere, similar symptoms can occur on the left side of the
body. Rather than have problems with reading and writing,
however, the person will have trouble copying and drawing.
Neglect, or lack of awareness, of objects in the left visual field

may also be present. Symptoms of a pure motor stroke, which results from a lesion in the internal capsule or the base of the pons, are unilateral weakness of the arms, legs, and face with no changes in visual, sensory, or cognitive functions. Pure sensory stroke due to a lesion to the thalamus (the relay station for the senses) results in unilateral numbness of the arms, legs, and face, with no weakness or visual or cognitive dysfunction. Different sets of symptoms may be present for lesions in other areas of the brain.

TRAUMATIC BRAIN INJURY

Traumatic brain injury (TBI) is damage to the brain that comes from some type of blow or penetrating injury to the head or as a result of acceleration-deceleration forces. Each year, at least 1.4 million cases of TBI are treated at emergency rooms and hospitals in the United States and are the cause of 50,000 deaths

THE INSPIRING STORY OF CHRISTOPHER REEVE

Perhaps best known for portraying the comic book hero in the *Superman* movies, Christopher Reeve became famous and respected worldwide for a very different reason. In 1995, Reeve suffered a severe SCI during a horseback riding competition. Although the injury left him completely paralyzed from the neck down, he quickly became an international spokesman for research into ways to treat and perhaps someday cure SCIs. In 1999, Reeve founded the Christopher Reeve Paralysis Foundation (CRPS), which works to promote research and provides funding to improve the lives of people who have been disabled by SCIs. As the CRPS Web site explains, ". . . Reeve has not only put a human face on spinal cord injury but he has motivated neuroscientists around the world to conquer the most complex diseases of the brain and central nervous system." Sadly, Reeve died in October 2004 from complications of a pressure wound infection.

and about 99,000 long-term disabilities, including 20,000 cases of epilepsy. There are probably many additional cases of mild TBI that go unreported and even unrecognized. TBI is responsible for one-third to one-half of all traumatic deaths and is the major cause of disabling symptoms in people under the age of 45. TBI is also the leading cause of death for children and adolescents. The incidence of TBI is twice as high in males as in females. According to the Centers for Disease Control, the leading causes of TBI are falls (28%), motor vehicle accidents (20%), struck-by or -against accidents (19%), and assaults (11%). Most of the estimated 1.6 to 3.8 million cases of TBI that occur during sports and other recreational activities are mild and are not treated at an emergency room or a hospital. Motor vehicle accidents result in the most hospitalizations for TBI, and firearms are the leading cause of deaths from TBI (9 out of 10 victims die). The use of seat belts, helmets, and child restraints has reduced the incidence of TBI—except for those resulting from firearms, which are on the increase.

Diffuse axonal injury (DAI) is the major cause of injury in up to 50% of TBIs that require hospitalization, and it also causes 35% of TBI-related deaths. If the victim loses consciousness, doctors assume that DAI has occurred. There does not have to be physical impact for DAI to result. Whiplash from an automobile accident, for example, can be severe enough to kill a person. Rapid acceleration and deceleration of the brain causes a shearing motion of axonal cytoplasm. This can damage the axons and cause them to degenerate, a process which may continue for months to years after the injury. Neuronal cell bodies and glial cells may also degenerate due to secondary processes.

Symptoms that may result from TBI include hearing loss, vertigo (dizziness due to inner ear damage), impairment of olfaction, vision problems such as double vision, seizures, chronic headaches, tremors, spasticity, irritability and agitation, aggressiveness, impulsivity, depression, problems with motor coordination and speed, personality changes, problems with speech, retrograde amnesia (loss of previous memory), anterograde amnesia (loss of the ability to form new memories), slowing of information processing speed, concentration problems, and other cognitive dysfunction, such as problems with planning, reasoning, and judgment. It is estimated that 10% of all cases of epilepsy result from TBI. Acute (immediate) symptoms may include headache, nausea, confusion, agitation, and disorientation.

DEMENTIAS

Dementia is a disease primarily associated with aging. It is rarely seen in people younger than 60. The various types of dementia are characterized by the pathological changes to brain tissue and by the resulting cognitive and behavioral changes. Because dementias represent a progressive deterioration of the brain, they are all eventually fatal. As the number of people over the age of 60 increases due to improvements in health care and lifestyles, the number of people with some form of dementia will grow, making these disorders a major challenge to medical professionals and an important focus for research efforts.

Alzheimer's disease (AD) is the most common form of dementia in people over age 60. It currently affects 4 million people in the United States alone. A small percentage of AD cases are seen in patients under 60; these cases are known as early onset AD and are thought to result from specific inherited mutations in genes located on chromosomes 1, 14, and 21. Many patients with Down syndrome, which is characterized by an extra copy of chromosome 21, develop AD by the time they reach middle age. Late onset AD, which represents the rest of AD cases, occurs in victims older than 60. It is believed to result from susceptibility to one or more risk factors, including environmental factors. The length of time between diagnosis and death can vary from 5 to 20 years.

The progressive dementia of AD begins as a subtle change in declarative memory, caused by gradual damage to the brain structures involved in cognitive processes. As the disease progresses, symptoms become more pronounced. Mood swings, language deterioration, personality changes, poor judgment, and confusion become more severe as the disease progresses. Eventually, the patient loses the ability to speak, becomes bedridden, and dies. MRI (magnetic resonance imaging) studies have revealed that neurodegeneration in AD begins in the entorhinal cortex and spreads to the hippocampus and other limbic areas of the temporal lobe, then moves on to higher-order association cortices (Figure 10.3). Sensorimotor and sensory areas of the cortex are spared. The neuropathology of AD is characterized by *amyloid plaques* and *neurofibrillary tangles*. Beta-amyloid protein is overproduced in AD and is deposited between the neurons. *Tau protein* is a normal component of microtubules, hollow cytoskeletal components that transport materials produced in the soma to the axon and dendrites. In AD, tau protein dissociates from microtubules and accumulates as neurofibrillary tangles inside diseased neurons. Subunits of failed microfilaments, organelles that normally provide structural support to the cell, accumulate to form small structures called *inclusion bodies*. Inclusion bodies are found in AD cases in which there are signs of parkinsonism (motor problems that resemble those present in Parkinson's disease) as well as in some of the other dementias.

Vascular dementia, the second most common type of dementia, is caused by damage to the brain resulting from one large stroke or multiple small ones. The latter is known as *multi-infarct dementia*. Symptoms vary depending on where the lesion is located in the brain. Autopsies of many patients who had vascular dementia also show neuropathological changes like those associated with AD. About 30% of AD patients also have lesions caused by stroke.

Pick's Disease (PcD) is characterized by *Pick bodies*, cytoplasmic inclusions made up of tau protein fibrils that range in size from one-half to two times that of the nucleus and displace the nucleus from its normal position in the cell. PcD is also

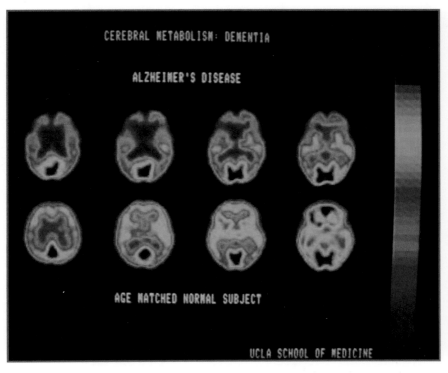

Figure 10.3 Alzheimer's disease causes impairment of cognition. These PET scans, taken during a research study, show the brains of an Alzheimer's patient and a healthy patient of the same age. Age-matched normal controls have higher levels of cerebral metabolism. The more active areas are "lit up" with color that changes with the intensity of the radioactivity, such as red for the most active areas, yellow for the next most active areas, and so on. A reduced level of cerebral metabolism is evidence of reduced activity of neurons. This lowered level of metabolism could be due to the loss of neurons that is characteristic of Alzheimer's. It could also be partly due to impaired function of the remaining the neurons.

characterized by ballooned, or swollen, neurons, termed *Pick cells*. There is atrophy or shrinking of the frontal and/or temporal lobes, with or without atrophy of the parietal cortex. Behavioral and personality changes such as aggressiveness, agitation, loss of inhibition, apathy, impulsivity, and impaired judgment are early symptoms of PcD. **Anomia**, or word-finding difficulty, is a language impairment that is present early in the disease. Explicit memory impairment is the primary initial symptom of AD. In PcD, explicit memory impairment is less pronounced, as is impairment of visuospatial function. As PcD progresses, all cognitive functions decline. A rapid decline in expressive language, resulting in aphasia, is diagnostic of PcD.

Prion diseases are neurodegenerative diseases caused by abnormally folded proteins called **prions**, also known as "slow viruses." Prions are resistant to enzymatic deactivation because they do not possess nucleic acids as do viruses and other infectious agents. When examined with a microscope, the brain of a person with prion disease is seen to have a *spongiform encephalopathy*, in which vacuoles (tiny, fluid-filled cavities) fill the neuronal cytoplasm and make the damaged tissue look porous like a sponge. Symptoms may not appear for 1 to 20 years, but once the disease is active, there is rapidly progressive dementia followed by death. There may also be ataxia due to cerebellar degeneration. Prion disease can be inherited, infectious, or sporadic (of unknown cause). Inherited, or familial, prion disease is genetic. There are 20 known genetic mutations that cause prion disease. One of these is classic Creutzfeldt-Jakob disease (cCJD). *Infectious,* or *acquired,* prion disease is transmitted by eating infected tissues or from medical procedures that use infected tissues. The latter include dura mater transplants, corneal transplants, and the use of hormones from infected pituitaries. Depth electrodes that have not been properly sterilized have also been known to transmit cCJD. *Sporadic prion disease* may be due to a spontaneous mutation or to one of the other two causes but without evidence of causation.

Variant Creutzfeldt-Jakob disease (vCJD), also known as "mad cow" disease, is thought to be a rare human variant of bovine spongiform encephalopathy (BSE). There is strong evidence that the disease may be spread from cattle to humans. Compared with cCJD, the median age at time of death is much younger—28 years as opposed to 68 years.

In animals with BSE, prion protein accumulates in the spinal cord, brain, retina, dorsal root ganglia, bone marrow, and distal ileum (small intestine). If these tissues make their way into ground feed that is fed to other animals, the disease can be transmitted. Cattle and sheep are the only animals known to be susceptible to the disease. Eating muscle meats and avoiding ground meats, such as sausage and burgers, helps one to avoid ingestion of potentially infected tissues. However, it might be advisable to avoid these meats entirely when traveling in areas where an outbreak of BSE has been known to occur.

Thiamine deficiency (which can result from excessive alcohol intake, malnutrition, dialysis, severe morning sickness with vomiting during pregnancy, or prolonged administration of intravenous fluids without vitamins) can cause Wernicke-Korsakoff syndrome. About 10% of chronic alcoholics develop Wernicke-Korsakoff syndrome. Wernicke's syndrome is the early, or acute, stage of the disorder, and Korsakoff's amnesic syndrome is the chronic phase of the disorder. Wernicke's syndrome is characterized by ataxia, paralysis of certain eye muscles, and confusion. Hemorrhagic lesions of the walls of the cerebral aqueduct and the third and fourth ventricles may appear. At this stage of the disease, therapy with thiamine replacement can reverse most of the symptoms, although half of the patients who recover continue to have trouble walking. Left untreated, Wernicke's syndrome eventually leads to coma and death. In fact, 15 to 20% of patients who are hospitalized for Wernicke's syndrome do not survive.

As the disease progresses to the Korsakoff's stage, there is bilateral degeneration of the mammillary bodies, the septal nuclei, and the midline thalamic nuclei, which may include the dorsomedial nucleus and the anterior nucleus. Loss of hippocampal volume comparable with that seen in AD may also play a role in the amnesic symptoms of the disease. These midline structures surrounding the ventricles are more susceptible to toxins, such as alcohol, dissolved in the cerebrospinal fluid. Atrophy of other brain areas, including the cerebellum, occur as well. Severe impairments of anterograde and sometimes retrograde memory occur with the Korsakoff's stage of the disease. Patients tend to make up stories to fill in memory gaps. They seem to be unaware of their memory loss. Although recovery is much slower than with Wernicke's, treatment with thiamine will reverse some of the symptoms, but the memory loss is irreversible. Frequently, supervised living conditions are necessary for Korsakoff's patients.

PREVENTING BRAIN DISEASE

Scientists have found that the foods we eat, the amount of exercise we get, our level of mental activity, and even the air we breathe can affect the way our brains function. Free radicals, or molecules with unpaired electrons, are generated during normal cellular functions. **Antioxidant** enzymes in the body, as well as antioxidants in food, normally do a good job in neutralizing free radicals before they steal electrons from DNA, cell membranes, and other cellular constituents and damaged cells. However, if antioxidant defenses are low or free radicals are produced at a rate higher than these defenses can handle, disease can result. Free radicals are thought to be involved in aging processes and in a number of diseases, including Parkinson's disease and AD. Eating lots of dark or brightly colored fruits and vegetables and taking antioxidant supplements are good ways to protect the brain from free radicals. Other nutrients, including omega-3 fatty acids and the B vitamins, have also been shown to be important for brain health. Regular exercise not only increases cerebral blood flow but has been shown to increase neurogenesis. Mental activity increases synaptic connections and helps provide a reserve of these connections as the brain ages. Avoiding toxins in the water supply and the environment also helps protect the brain. How well we take care of our brains can make a big difference in how well it functions and resists aging and disease processes.

CONNECTIONS

Damage to the nervous system resulting from trauma or disease can have devastating effects. Loss of function due to damage of structures and pathways in the neuromuscular system can cripple a person. Autoimmune disease may attack receptors at neuromuscular junctions or the myelin of axons. Depending on where the damage takes place, degeneration of structures in the basal ganglia can produce inhibition or disinhibition of movement. Cerebellar damage can lead to problems with balance and gait. Epilepsy can cause twitches or convulsions of muscles, but it starts in the cerebral cortex and is caused by too many groups of neurons firing at the same time. Injury and disease of areas in the temporal, frontal, and parietal lobes can result in severe cognitive impairments. Injury to the brain due to stroke or trauma causes an enormous loss of life and a large number of disabling conditions each year. Dementias are usually progressive neurodegenerative diseases that affect the elderly. However, dementia can happen at an earlier age if the person experiences trauma, infection, autoimmune disease, or genetic problems. To date, scientists have not found cures for most nervous system impairments. Preventive measures in the form of improved diet, regular exercise, and safety precautions are one way to help prevent the disorders. Rehabilitative therapy for both physical and cognitive impairments may also help people who are affected. Continued research to understand the disease processes involved may yield an understanding of how to stop them. Again, those answers may be related to the normal physiological processes that maintain the health of the nervous system.

Appendix: Conversion Chart

Unit (metric)		Metric to English	English to Metric	
LENGTH				
Kilometer	km	1 km 0.62 mile (mi)	1 mile (mi)	1.609 km
Meter	m	1 m 3.28 feet (ft)	1 foot (ft)	0.305 m
Centimeter	cm	1 cm 0.394 inches (in)	1 inch (in)	2.54 cm
Millimeter	mm	1 mm 0.039 inches (in)	1 inch (in)	25.4 mm
Micrometer	μm	1 - millionth of a meter		
WEIGHT (MASS)				
Kilogram	kg	1 kg 2.2 pounds (lbs)	1 pound (lbs)	0.454 kg
Gram	g	1 g 0.035 ounces (oz)	1 ounce (oz)	28.35 g
Milligram	mg	1 mg 0.000035 ounces (oz)		
Microgram	μg	1 - millionth of a gram		
VOLUME				
Liter	L	1 L 1.06 quarts	1 gallon (gal)	3.785 L
			1 quart (qt)	0.94 L
			1 pint (pt)	0.47 L
Milliliter	mL or cc	1 mL 0.034 fluid ounce (fl oz)	1 fluid ounce (fl oz)	29.57 mL
Microliter	μL	1 - millionth of a liter		
TEMPERATURE				
		$[°F] = [°C] \times 9/5 + 32$	$[°C] = ([°F] - 32) \times 5/9$	

Glossary

Acetylcholine Neurotransmitter released by preganglionic autonomic neurons, motor neurons, postganglionic parasympathetic neurons, certain nuclei in the brainstem and basal forebrain, and interneurons in various brain structures.

Action potential Electrical impulse produced by depolarization of the neuronal membrane; can stimulate impulses in adjacent neurons or contraction of adjacent muscle fiber.

Adenohypophysis Anterior lobe of the pituitary gland; synthesizes and releases hormones into the bloodstream.

Adrenal medulla The inner layer of the adrenal gland; releases norepinephrine and epinephrine when activated.

Ageusia A total loss of taste sensation.

Agonist Drug that mimics the action of a neurotransmitter at its receptor.

Alpha rhythms Electrical activities in the brain that create regular brain waves at a rate of 8 to 12 cycles per second.

Alpha motor neurons Neurons in ventral gray matter of the spinal cord; axon branches synapse on muscle fibers and transmit the signals that causes them to contract.

Amygdala Limbic system structure important in the regulation of emotion; found in the medial temporal lobe.

Amygdalofugal pathway Input/output pathway for the basolateral and central nuclear divisions of the amygdala.

Anomia Impairment in word finding or the retrieval of specific words.

Anosmia A complete loss of the sense of smell.

Antagonist Drug, neurotransmitter, or other chemical that binds to a receptor and blocks the action of a neurotransmitter.

Anterior Toward the front.

Anterior commissure   Fiber bundle that links the temporal cortices of the two hemispheres; a few anterior fibers link olfactory structures of the two hemispheres.

Anterograde amnesia   Loss of the ability to remember new information.

Antidiuretic hormone (ADH)   See *vasopressin*.

Antioxidant   Chemical that blocks the oxidation process by neutralizing free radicals; natural antioxidants include vitamin C, vitamin E, vitamin A, and bioflavonoids. Enzymes that act as antioxidants include catalase, superoxide dismutase, and glutathione peroxidase.

Apraxia   Problems performing learned skilled movements due to damage to the brain.

Aqueous humor   Fluid that circulates in the space between the cornea and the lens of the eye.

Arachnoid membrane   The meningeal layer between the dura mater and the pia mater of the brain and spinal cord.

Arachnoid trabeculae   Spidery extensions between the arachnoid membrane and the pia mater.

Ascending reticular activating system (ARAS)   Fiber pathway consisting of axons of cholinergic, dopaminergic, serotinergic, and noradrenergic brainstem nuclei; activates the cerebral cortex.

Association area   Area of the cerebral cortex that associates and integrates sensory and/or motor information from primary areas.

Associative learning   See *classical conditioning*.

Astrocyte   Glial cell that provides nutritional and structural support for neurons.

Ataxia   Uncoordinated movements associated with cerebellar damage or impairment of cerebellar function due to intoxication.

Autoimmune disease   Disease that results when the immune system attacks one of the body's own proteins as if it were a foreign protein.

Autonomic nervous system   Division of the peripheral nervous system that controls the body's vital processes, such as heart rate, blood pressure, and rate of respiration.

Axon   Neuronal process (extension) that carries impulses away from the cell body toward another neuron.

Axon hillock   The place where the cell body meets the axon and action potentials are generated.

Basal ganglia   A group of subcortical nuclei that lie beneath the lateral ventricles in the forebrain. Through their interconnections with the thalamus and cerebral cortex, they participate in the motivation, planning, and execution of movements.

Basic rest-activity cycle (BRAC)   A proposed 90-minute cycle of rest and activity that occurs throughout the day and continues through the night as the sleep cycle.

Bed nucleus of the stria terminalis   Thin C-shaped amygdalar nucleus that follows the stria terminalis as it follows the C-shape of the caudate nucleus; its functions are similar to those of the central amygdalar nuclei.

Beta rhythms   Electrical brain activities in which brain waves occur irregularly at a rate of 13 to 30 cycles per second.

Bipolar cell   A bipolar neuron found in the middle, or bipolar, layer of the retina; transmits visual information from the photoreceptor cells to the ganglion cells.

Bipolar neuron   A neuron that has two processes, a dendrite and an axon, that arise from opposite ends of the cell body; most bipolar neurons are sensory neurons.

Blood-brain barrier   Structures that protect the brain by preventing most substances in the blood from entering the brain; includes the tight junctions of the endothelial lining of the brain capillaries.

Brainstem   Area of the brain extending from the diencephalon to the junction of the brain with the spinal cord; includes the medulla, pons, and midbrain.

Broca's area   Area in the left inferior (lower) frontal lobe that is involved in the production of speech. Also called the motor speech area.

Calcarine fissure (or sulcus)   A deep infolding of the cerebral cortex from the tip of the occipital lobe to near the posterior end of the corpus callosum; the primary visual cortex covers the banks of this fissure.

Cardiac muscle Type of muscle found only in the walls of the heart; resembles striated muscle in appearance but is not under voluntary control; responsible for the heart's contractions.

Caudal   Toward the tail end.

Caudate nucleus   One of the input nuclei of the basal ganglia; C-shaped structure that lies close to the lateral ventricle and forms the lateral wall and floor of the body of the lateral ventricle. It is involved in cognition and the control of eye movements.

Cell body   The enlarged part of a neuron that contains the nucleus and cell organelles; also called the soma.

Cell membrane   The membrane that surrounds the cell and controls the passage of materials into and out of the cell; the plasma membrane.

Cell theory   Theory that states that cells are the basic unit of structure in all living things.

Central nervous system (CNS)   The brain and spinal cord.

Cerebellum   Convoluted brain structure that lies dorsal to the brainstem and covers the fourth ventricle; involved in motor skill learning, posture, and planning and coordinating movement. It may also be involved in higher cognitive processes.

Cerebral cortex   Thin (1.5- to 4.5-mm [0.06-to 0.18-in]) layer of gray matter covering the cerebral hemispheres. Contains primary sensory and primary motor areas, unimodal association areas for the individual senses, multimodal association areas for the integration of sensory information from different senses, and limbic areas.

Cerebrum   The largest part of the brain, consisting of two cerebral hemispheres, and covered by a thin layer of gray matter—the cerebral cortex. See *cerebral cortex*.

Choroid   The darkly pigmented layer between the sclera and the retina that provides nourishment to the retina.

Circadian pacemaker   The suprachiasmatic nucleus (SCN); controls the timing of the sleep/wake cycle and the daily rhythms of physiological functions.

Classical conditioning   A type of learning in which a previously neutral stimulus becomes associated with a stimulus that naturally produces a response.

Cochlea   The snail-shaped part of the inner ear that contains the organ of Corti, the organ of hearing.

Commissure   A bundle of nerve fibers that connects paired nervous system structures.

Cones   Receptor cells in the retina responsible for high-acuity vision and color vision; cones are most active in bright light.

Consolidation   Process by which information is stored in memory; appears to involve synaptic changes.

Corticobulbar tract   Fiber pathway from the motor cortices (upper motor neurons) to the motor nuclei (lower motor neurons) of the cranial nerves and to associated interneurons in the reticular formation.

Corticospinal tract   Fiber pathway from the motor cortices (upper motor neurons) to the motor neurons (lower motor neurons) in the spinal cord. Divides into the lateral corticospinal tract and the ventral corticospinal tract just above the spinal cord at the pyramidal decussation in the medulla.

Contralateral   On the opposite side of the body.

Cornea   Transparent, dome-shaped structure that covers the front of the eye; helps focus light rays on the retina.

Corpus callosum   Nervous connection (commissure) between the two cerebral hemispheres.

Cranial nerves   Twelve pairs of nerves that are sensory, motor, or both; they control the activities of the head and neck.

Cribriform plate   Part of the ethmoid bone that is directly above the nasal cavity; contains tiny perforations through which the axons of the primary olfactory neurons pass from the nasal cavity up to the olfactory bulb at the base of the brain.

Cytoplasm   The thick, semiliquid substance that fills the interior of a cell.

Declarative memory   Explicit memory; memory that is conscious and can be put into words; includes episodic and semantic memory.

Deep sleep   See *slow-wave sleep.*

Dementia   Loss of cognitive functions due to disease of or damage to brain structures or pathways.

Dendrites   Small branchlike extensions from one side of the cell body of a neuron; located at the opposite end of the cell from the axon. They receive impulses from other neurons and carry them toward the cell body.

Dendritic spine   Small budlike extension of a dendrite on which the terminal button of another neuron synapses.

Dentate gyrus   One of the structures that make up the hippocampal formation.

Desynchronized sleep   See *REM sleep.*

Diencephalon   The thalamus and hypothalamus.

Dopamine   Monoamine neurotransmitter of the catecholamine subclass.

Dorsal   Toward the back top side of the brain.

Dorsal root ganglion   Cluster of cell bodies of bipolar neurons whose dendrites bring sensory information from the periphery and whose axons transmit that information to the central nervous system; found in the dorsal root of each spinal nerve.

Dorsomedial thalamic nucleus   Relay nucleus to the prefrontal association cortex for the amygdala, basal ganglia, hypothalamus, and olfactory system. Relays temperature, pain, and itch information to anterior cingulate gyrus, and has direct reciprocal connections with the prefrontal cortex. Involved in emotions, learning and memory, and cognition.

Dura mater   Tough outer meningeal layer of the brain and spinal cord; lines the skull and vertebral canal.

Eardrum   See *tympanic membrane.*

Electroencephalogram (EEG)   Paper or electronic record of electrical activity of the brain; obtained using electrodes pasted to the scalp.

Electromyogram (EMG)   Record of muscle activity recorded using electrodes either on the skin or inserted directly into muscle tissue.

Electro-oculogram (EOG)   Record of eye movements recorded using electrodes attached near the eyes.

Embolism   Blockage of a blood vessel by a clot or other material carried in the bloodstream from another area of the body.

Encoding   Process by which stimuli from the environment are changed into a neural code that can be perceived by the brain.

Endogenous opioids   Neurotransmitters, such as enkephalins, dynorphins, and endorphins, that are produced by the brain and bind to the same receptors as heroin, morphine, and other opiates.

Enteric nervous system (ENS)   The neuronal network within the walls of the gastrointestinal tract that operates independently of the central nervous system; classified as a division of the autonomic nervous system.

Ependymal cells   A type of glial cell that forms the ependymal layer that lines the ventricles of the brain.

Episodic learning   Learning that involves remembering events and the order in which they occur.

Episodic memory   Memory of events and the order in which they occur.

Explicit memory   See *declarative memory*.

Extensor   A muscle that, when it contracts, straightens a limb .

Extracellular fluid   The fluid that surrounds cells; has different concentrations of ions than intracellular fluid.

Extrafusal muscle fibers   Muscle fibers involved in skeletal movement.

Flexor   A muscle that, when it contracts, causes a limb to bend.

Foramen magnum   Opening at the base of the skull through which the spinal cord passes.

Fornix   Input/output pathway between the hippocampus and the septal nuclei and hypothalamus.

Fovea   Small area at the center of the retina where light focuses; contains only cones, and vision is sharpest there.

Free nerve endings   Nonencapsulated receptors distributed throughout the body; they detect pain and temperature (the majority), tickle sensations, pressure, crude touch, and possibly heat and cold.

Frontal lobe   The part of each cerebral hemisphere that is found in front of the central sulcus and above the lateral sulcus.

Gamma-amino butyric acid (GABA)   An amino acid transmitter in the brain that inhibits the firing of neurons.

Gamma motor neurons   Small motor neurons that synapse on intrafusal muscle fibers (stretch receptors) and adjust their sensitivity.

Ganglion (plural: *ganglia*)   Group of neurons with similar functions found in the peripheral nervous system; plural, ganglia

Ganglion cells   Neurons found in the outermost layer of the retina; their axons come together at the back of the eye to form the optic nerve.

Glia   Cells of the central nervous system that provide support functions for neurons.

Globus pallidus   One of the basal ganglia medial to the putamen (closer to the midline); sends most of the outputs of the basal ganglia.

Glutamate   The most common excitatory neurotransmitter in the brain.

Golgi tendon organ   An encapsulated receptor that detects muscle tension.

Gray matter   Areas of the brain and spinal cord where there are many neurons, which give the tissue a grayish color.

Hemispheric dominance   Lateralization of function; the dominant role of one or the other cerebral hemisphere in a particular function.

Hippocampal commissure   Fiber tract that interconnects the two hippocampi.

Hippocampus   Structure in the temporal lobe of the cerebrum associated with emotion and memory.

Hyperpolarization   Influx of negative ions that increases the membrane potential of a neuron and decreases the probability of an action potential.

Hypnagogic hallucination   Dreamlike sights, sounds, or smells that occur just before falling asleep or just after awakening. Represents the occurrence of REM (rapid eye movement) sleep accompanied by sleep paralysis during a waking state.

Hypogeusia   A partial loss of the sense of taste.

Hyposmia   A partial loss of the sense of smell.

Hypothalamic-pituitary-adrenal (HPA) axis   Refers to the series of hormones produced by the hypothalamus, pituitary, and adrenal gland during the stress response. Corticotropin-releasing hormone (CRH) released by the hypothalamus stimulates the release of adrenocorticotropic-releasing hormone (ACTH) by the pituitary. ACTH then stimulates the release of cortisol from the adrenal cortex.

Hypothalamus   Group of nuclei located beneath the thalamus in the diencephalon; involved in control of multiple physiological and endocrine functions.

Immediate memory   See *short-term memory.*

Implicit memory   Nondeclarative memory, or memory that is less accessible to conscious recollection and verbal retrieval.

Indirect agonists   Chemicals that increase the level of neurotransmitter in the synapse.

Instrumental conditioning   A form of stimulus-response learning in which the learner associates a particular behavior with a reward or punishment; behaviors that are rewarded increase and behaviors that are punished decrease.

Insula   Area of the cerebral cortex found at the floor of the lateral fissure; covered by the opercula of the frontal and temporal lobes.

Insular cortex   The area of the cortex at the floor of the lateral fissure.

Intention tremor   Shaking of a limb while the limb is in motion.

Intervertebral foramen (plural: *intervertebral foramina*)   Opening between two vertebrae through which a spinal nerve exits.

Intrafusal muscle fibers   Stretch receptors that contain fibers innervated by sensory and motor nerve endings; attached at either end to extrafusal muscle fibers.

Inverse agonist   Drug that binds to a receptor and has the opposite effect to that of the endogenous neurotransmitter.

Involuntary muscle   Muscle that is not under conscious control; smooth muscle and cardiac muscle.

Ipsilateral   On the same side of the body.

Iris   The pigmented, muscular structure that controls the size of the pupil and gives the eyes their color.

Kinesthesia   The sense that makes us aware of body movements; uses information received from receptors in the muscles, tendons, and joints.

Lateral geniculate nucleus   Thalamic nucleus to which the optic tract projects.

Lateralization of function   See *hemispheric dominance*.

Lens   Transparent structure suspended behind the iris of the eye that focuses light on the retina.

Level of injury   The most caudal vertebral segment below which there is a partial or complete absence of sensation and movement on both sides of the body.

Limbic system   Interconnected diencephalic and telencephalic nuclei that are involved in emotions and memory and that regulate ingestive, aggressive, and reproductive behaviors. Structures include the hippocampus, amygdala, septal nuclei, hypothalamus, olfactory bulb, olfactory cortex, and limbic cortex.

Long-term memory   Memory that is stored in the brain for a long time—as long as a lifetime. It has an enormous capacity and includes all the knowledge we have learned and all the events of our lives.

Lumbar cistern   The space in the lower vertebral canal that is not occupied by the spinal cord but instead by spinal nerves that descend from the spinal cord to exit their appropriate intervertebral foramina. This area is where the needle is inserted for a spinal tap.

Macula   Area in the center of the retina where light focuses and where cones are the most heavily concentrated.

Medial geniculate nucleus   Nucleus in the thalamus to which auditory information goes before it is relayed to the primary auditory cortex.

Median forebrain bundle   Fiber pathway through which axons of brainstem nuclei ascend and descend between brainstem nuclei and the cerebral cortex as well as subcortical nuclei. The fibers of the ascending reticular activating system (ARAS) travel up this pathway, and projections from the hypothalamus to the autonomic nervous system travel down this pathway.

Medulla oblongata   Most posterior region of the hindbrain (brainstem); transitions to the spinal cord at the foramen magnum.

Meissner's corpuscles   Elongated encapsulated receptors located just beneath the epidermis in hairless skin, especially in the hands and feet; numerous in the fingertips. Together with Merkel endings, responsible for fine tactile (touch) discrimination.

Meninges   Protective membranes that surround and cover the brain and spinal cord.

Merkel's disk   Nonencapsulated touch receptor with a disk-shaped terminal that inserts into a Merkel cell in the basal layer of the epidermis of both hairless and hairy skin; found in between hair follicles in hairy skin.

Microglia   Smallest glial cells; engulf and destroy invading microbes, clean up debris after brain injury, and secrete growth factors and cytokines.

Midbrain   Most anterior region of the hindbrain (brainstem), located just beneath the diencephalon.

Middle ear   Air-filled region between the eardrum and the inner ear. A chain of three tiny bones (ossicles) transmit vibrations from the eardrum to the oval window of the cochlea.

Monoamine oxidases   Brain and liver enzymes that break down the monoamine neurotransmitters serotonin, dopamine, and norepinephrine.

Monoamines   A group of neurotransmitters that includes serotonin, norepinephrine, and dopamine.

Motor learning   The learning of skilled movements such as knitting, playing a musical instrument, or riding a bicycle; the movements become automatic over time.

Motor unit   A unit including a motor neuron, its axons and dendrites, and the muscle fibers that it innervates.

Movement decomposition   A condition that can result from damage to the cerebellum; movements that are normally smooth decompose into a jerky series of discrete movements.

Multipolar neuron   Neuron that has multiple dendritic trees and one long axon. Most neurons, including motor neurons and pyramidal cells, are of this type.

Muscle endplate   The specialized area on the membrane of a muscle fiber on which the axon terminal of a motor neuron synapses; nicotinic cholinergic receptors are found inside the folds that increase the surface area of the synapse.

Muscle spindles   Long, thin stretch receptors found scattered among muscle fibers; they detect changes in muscle length.

Myelin   Insulating covering formed by the concentric wrapping of oligodendrocyte or Schwann cell processes around an axon; increases the conduction velocity of the axon.

Myofibrils   Filaments (chains) of myosin or actin molecules.

Narcolepsy   Sleep disorder in which a person is always sleepy during the daytime; short episodes of REM sleep during waking hours are characteristic of this disorder.

Neural tube   Embryonic precursor of the nervous system; cells lining the neural tube become neurons and glia, and the tube's cavity becomes the ventricular system and spinal canal.

Neurogenesis   Production of new neurons from stem cells. Long thought to be absent in the adult brain of humans, but now known to occur in the hippocampus and in the lining of the lateral ventricles.

Neuromuscular junction   Synapse between alpha motor neuron and muscle fiber; includes presynaptic motor terminal, synaptic cleft, and muscle endplate.

Neuron   Nerve cell; the functional and structural unit of the nervous system.

Neuron theory   The belief that the nervous system is made up of cells, in contrast to the reticular theory.

Neuropeptide   Short peptide that functions as a neurotransmitter; cleaved from larger precursor protein and transported from cell body to axon terminal.

Neurotransmitter   Chemical messenger of the nervous system that binds to a specific receptor and activates it.

Nociceptor   Pain receptor that consists of free nerve endings that receive and transmit information about harmful stimuli.

Node of Ranvier   Gap between myelin wrappings of glial processes around the axon.

Nondeclarative memory   Stored information that is not available to conscious thought and is difficult to explain in words.

NonREM sleep   The four stages of sleep that precede REM (rapid eye movement) sleep.

Norepinephrine   A monamine neurotransmitter of the catecholamine subclass that is produced and released by all sympathetic postganglionic neurons except those that innervate the sweat glands, by brainstem nuclei, and by the adrenal medulla (as a hormone).

Nucleus (plural: *nuclei*)   In cells, the control center of the cell, which contains the chromosomes; in the central nervous system, a group of neurons with a similar function.

Nucleus accumbens   Structure in the ventral striatum that is formed by the fusion of the caudate nucleus and the putamen where they meet; serves as an interface between the limbic system and the motor system and is also important in addiction and substance abuse.

Observational learning   Learning by watching and mimicking the actions of others.

Occipital lobe   Posterior lobe of the brain containing the primary and association visual cortices.

Oculomotor loop   Anatomical loop from the areas in the frontal and parietal lobe that control eye movements to the substantia nigra (one of the basal ganglia), then to the ventral anterior thalamic nucleus and back to the prefrontal and higher-order visual cortices.

Olfaction   The sense of smell.

Olfactory receptors   Proteins on the surface of primary olfactory neurons that detect gaseous molecules in the air; receptors for the sense of smell.

Olfactory tract   The nerve pathway from the olfactory bulb to the primary olfactory cortex.

Oligodendrocyte   Glial cell that provides the myelin wrapping of axons in the central nervous system.

Optic chiasm   Area directly above the pituitary gland and directly below the hypothalamus where the nasal half of each optic nerve crosses to the contralateral side of the brain.

Optic radiation   Nerve pathway from the lateral geniculate nucleus back through the temporal lobe to the ipsilateral primary visual cortex.

Orbitofrontal cortex   Area of the prefrontal cortex found underneath the brain; it is the area of the frontal lobe that is most involved in emotions.

Organelles   Specialized structures in the cytoplasm that perform essential functions for the cell; most are surrounded by a membrane.

Organ of Corti   The sensory organ of the inner ear. Consists of the basal membrane hair cells, and tectorial membrane.

Osmolarity   A measure of the number of particles of a dissolved substance in liquid, such as plasma. Sodium, chloride, glucose, and urea are the substances that contribute the most to the osmolarity of plasma.

Osmoreceptors   Receptors that detect changes in the osmolarity of the blood.

Ossicles   The three tiny bones of the middle ear, called the malleus, incus, and stapes.

Outer ear   Consists of the pinna, ear canal, and tympanic membrane.

Oxytocin   Hypothalamic hormone that causes contraction of the uterus during labor and ejection of milk during nursing.

Pacinian corpuscles   Widespread encapsulated receptors that are particularly sensitive to vibration; they are found in subcutaneous tissue, especially in the hands and feet, but also in the internal organs, joint capsules, and membranes that line the internal cavity and support the organs.

Paraplegia   Injury of the spinal cord that results in a loss of sensation and movement that may occur anywhere from the middle of the chest down through the extremities.

Parasympathetic nervous system   A division of the autonomic nervous system that performs restorative and maintenance functions; preganglionic parasympathetic neurons are found in the brainstem and the sacral spinal cord. Both its preganglionic and postganglionic neurons release acetylcholine.

Parietal lobe   One of the four lobes of each cerebral hemisphere. It is bounded on the rear by the parieto-occipital sulcus, in the front by the central sulcus, and at the bottom by the lateral sulcus and an imaginary line that extends from the edge of the lateral sulcus and intersects at right angles with an imaginary line drawn from the parieto-occipital sulcus to the occipital notch.

Parieto-occipital sulcus   Sulcus that forms the boundary between the parietal lobe and the occipital lobe.

Partial agonists   Drugs that bind to receptors and produce smaller effects than an endogenous neurotransmitter would.

Perception   Interpretation by the brain of sensory stimuli that it receives from the sense organs.

Perceptual learning   A type of learning that allows us to recognize and identify stimuli and to learn the relationships between stimuli.

Periaqueductal gray area   Area of gray matter surrounding the cerebral aqueduct in the midbrain; important in suppression of pain transmission and behavioral expression of emotions.

Peripheral nervous system   All components of the nervous system that are not contained within the brain and spinal cord; includes the sensory neurons, autonomic ganglia, and peripheral nerves.

Photopigment   A pigment found in photoreceptor cells that, on exposure to light, undergoes chemical changes that cause ion channels in the membrane to open and generate an action potential.

Photoreceptor   Neuron in the innermost retinal layer that transduces light stimuli into neural signals.

Pia mater   Innermost and most delicate of the three meningeal layers surrounding the brain and spinal cord.

Pinna   The flap of skin and cartilage on the outside of the head that is usually thought of as the "ear."

Pituitary gland   Called the "master gland" because it secretes hormones that control the secretion of hormones by other endocrine glands.

Pons   Brainstem region that lies between the midbrain and the medulla and is overlain dorsally by the cerebellum.

Posterior   Toward the back.

Postganglionic fibers   Axons of postganglionic neurons that synapse on a target organ or tissue; they release acetylcholine (parasympathetic) or norepinephrine (sympathetic) from their axon terminals.

Potentiation   To strengthen or increase in effectiveness.

Prefrontal lobotomy   Surgical procedure in which either the dorsal connections of the orbitofrontal cortex to the cingulate gyrus or its ventral connections to the diencephalon and temporal lobes are severed; results in a loss of the ability to express emotions.

Primary olfactory neurons   Neurons in the nasal cavity that have olfactory receptors. Their axons go up through tiny openings in the cribriform plate of the ethmoid bone to synapse on neurons in the olfactory bulbs, which are located at the base of the brain.

Primary visual cortex   Area of the cerebral cortex to which raw visual data is transmitted to be processed; located inside the calcarine fissure in the cortex.

Prion   An abnormally folded protein that can cause and transmit disease when infected tissues are eaten. Sometimes called a "slow virus."

Procedural memory   Memories that result from learning of rules and motor skills; sometimes learned unconsciously.

Proprioception   Position sense.

Pseudounipolar neuron   A type of bipolar neuron that has a fused process that bifurcates a short distance from the cell body into an axon and a dendrite; the dorsal root ganglion cell is an example of a bipolar neuron.

Pupil   The opening at the center of the iris of the eye.

Putamen   A basal ganglia nucleus involved in the control of movements of the limbs and the trunk.

Quadriplegia   See *tetraplegia*.

Reflex   Involuntary response to a stimulus.

Refractory period   Period of a few milliseconds following an action potential during which another action potential cannot be generated (absolute refractory period) or can be generated only with a much greater depolarization (relative refractory period); results from inactivation of sodium channels.

Rehearsal   Repetition of information in short-term memory that increases the likelihood that it will be stored in long-term memory.

Relational learning   Learning that involves learning relationships between multiple stimuli; includes spatial learning, episodic learning, observational learning, and the more complex forms of perceptual learning.

REM sleep   Period of sleep characterized by rapid eye movements, muscle atonia, vivid storylike dreams, and electrical activity similar to that seen during the waking state.

Renshaw cell   Interneuron in the spinal cord that provides a negative feedback control for the alpha motor neuron.

Reticular formation   Loose network of neurons and their processes that occupies most of the tegmentum (floor) of the brainstem; it receives afferents from all the senses, projects profusely upward and downward in the central nervous sytem, and is involved in virtually all activities of the central nervous system.

Reticular theory   The belief that the nervous system is a network of cytoplasm with many nuclei but no individual cells.

Reticulospinal tract   Fiber tract that descends from the reticular formation to the spinal cord and participates in the control of automatic movements such as walking and running, in the maintenance of muscle tone and posture, and in the control of sneezing, coughing, and respiration.

Retina   Layer behind the vitreous humor and in front of the choroid; consists of three layers of neurons that are interconnected by interneurons.

Retrieval   The process by which information in the memory stores is accessed.

Retrograde amnesia   Loss of memory for events that occurred before a trauma to the brain.

Rods   Photoreceptors that are sensitive to light of low intensity and functions in dim light; they do not contain color pigments, so they produce vision in tones of gray.

Rostral   Toward the head.

Rubrospinal tract   Fiber tract that descends from the red nucleus down the contralateral brainstem and spinal cord; thought to be important in the control of the movements of arm and hand muscles, but not the muscles of the fingers.

Ruffini's corpuscles (or Ruffini's endings)   Encapsulated, cirgar-shaped receptors found in the dermis of hairy skin; they respond to stretch in the skin and to deep pressure.

Schwann cell   Glial cell that provides the myelin for peripheral nerves.

Sclera   The tough white membrane that covers most of the eyeball (except the cornea).

Secondary visual cortex   Area of cortex that is located on the outside of the calcarine fissure; it surrounds the primary visual cortex, which is located inside the calcarine fissure, and it processes the raw visual data that it receives from the primary visual cortex.

Semantic memory   Memory of factual knowledge as opposed to memory of events.

Sensation   Process of receiving information through the sense organs.

Sensory memory   First stage of memory, which holds information for only milliseconds or seconds.

Serotonin   A monamine neurotransmitter of the indoleamine subclass; released from the raphe nuclei in the brainstem and in other places in the brain as well.

Short-term memory   Second stage of memory, which can store seven (plus or minus two) items for a duration of seconds to minutes; also known as immediate memory.

Skeletal muscles   Voluntary muscles; they are usually attached at each end to two different bones. When they contract, they cause the limbs and other structures to move.

Slow-wave sleep   Stages 3 and 4 of nonREM sleep; also known as deep sleep.

Smooth muscle   Involuntary nonstriated muscle found in eye muscles that control pupil size and the shape of the lens; in the sphincters of the urinary bladder and anus; in the walls of the blood vessels; in the walls of the digestive, urinary, and reproductive tracts; and around the hair follicles. Smooth muscle is under the control of the autonomic nervous system.

Soma   See *cell body*.

Somatic nervous system   A division of the peripheral nervous system; consists of the axons of the motor neurons and the sensory neurons and their axons.

Somatosensory   Pertaining to the body senses: pain, touch, pressure, temperature, proprioreception, and kinesthesia.

Spatial learning   Learning about objects in the environment and their relative location to one another and to the learner.

Stimulus-response learning   Occurs when a particular response to a stimulus is learned. Includes classical conditioning and instrumental conditioning.

Storage   See *consolidation*.

Stressors   Stimuli that the brain perceives as a threat to the physical or emotional safety of the body or to its homeostasis (balance).

Stress response   Physiological response to a stressor; consists of the activation of the sympathetic nervous system, the noradrenergic system (locus coeruleus), and the HPA axis.

Stria terminalis   Input/output pathway for the corticomedial nuclear group of the amygdala; primary target is the hypothalamic ventromedial nucleus.

Subarachnoid space   Cerebrospinal fluid-filled space between the arachnoid membrane and the pia mater; provides cushioning for the brain and spinal cord.

Substantia nigra   A midbrain structure that is considered one of the basal ganglia; projects to the striatum through a dopaminergic pathway, which degenerates in Parkinson's disease.

Subthalamic nucleus   One of the basal ganglia. It has reciprocal connections with the putamen. Damage to this nucleus causes hemiballism, or ballistic movements, of the contralateral limbs.

Suprachiasmatic nucleus (SCN)   See *circadian pacemaker*.

Sympathetic nervous system (SNS)   Division of the autonomic nervous system that prepares the body for "fight or flight" in response to a stressor.

Synapse   The area where nerve impulses are transmitted from an axon terminal to the adjacent structure (nerve or muscle cell).

Synaptic cleft   The tiny space between two neurons across which the neurotransmitter released by the axon terminals of the presynaptic neuron travels to bind to receptors on the postsynaptic neuronal membrane.

Synchronized sleep   See *nonREM sleep*.

Synergistic   Working together as a group.

Taste bud   Onion-shaped taste organ that contains the taste receptor neurons; most are found on or around the taste papillae on the surface of the tongue.

Tectospinal tract   Fiber tract that arises in the superior colliculus and descends through the contralateral brainstem to the cervical spinal cord; it is involved in the control of trunk, shoulder, and neck movements, especially reflexive responses to auditory, visual, and possibly somatosensory stimuli. May be involved in the coordination of head and eye movements.

Temporal lobe   One of the four lobes of each cerebral hemisphere; its upper boundary is the lateral sulcus, and its posterior boundary is the occipital lobe.

Tetraplegia   Loss of sensation and movement in all four limbs due to an injury in the cervical spinal cord.

Thalamus   Group of nuclei located above the hypothalamus in the diencephalon; all sensory information except that of the olfactory sense relays here before being sent to the cortex.

Thermoreceptors   Receptors in the hypothalamus that sense changes in body temperature and send signals to the autonomic nervous system.

Transduction   The process by which sensory receptors convert mechanical, chemical, or physical stimuli into nerve signals.

Tympanic membrane   The eardrum, a membrane that covers the opening into the middle ear and vibrates in response to sound waves that enter the outer ear.

Unipolar neuron   A neuron that has only one process, an axon, which has multiple terminals; because there are no dendrites, the cell body receives all incoming information.

Vasoconstriction   Narrowing or constriction of blood vessels. Activation of the sympathetic nervous system causes vasoconstriction.

Vasopressin   Antidiuretic hormone (ADH); causes the kidneys to reabsorb more water and decrease urine production and also causes vasoconstriction, which produces an increase in blood pressure.

Ventral   Referring to the front, or abdominal, side.

Ventricles   Cavities within the brain that are filled with cerebrospinal fluid secreted by the choroid plexus.

Ventricular system   The continuous system of ventricles in the brain through which the cerebrospinal fluid circulates.

Vermis   Midline structure that connects the two hemispheres of the cerebellum.

Vestibule The middle cavity of the bony labyrinth of the inner ear; lies between the semicircular canals and the cochlea and contains the vestibular sacs: the saccule and the utricle.

Vestibulospinal tracts Two motor pathways from the vestibular nucleus to the spinal cord. The lateral vestibulospinal tract descends to all levels of the spinal cord and is important in the control of posture and balance. The medial vestibulospinal tract descends to the cervical and upper thoracic spinal cord and participates in the control of head position.

Vitreous humor The gel-like substance that fills the back of the eye and maintains the shape of the eyeball.

Voluntary muscles Skeletal muscles; muscles that are under conscious control—they can be made to contract and relax at will.

Wernicke's area Area located posterior to the primary auditory area of the left temporal lobe. Damage to this area results in impairment in language comprehension.

White matter Areas of the brain where fiber tracts predominate. These areas have a whitish appearance due to the myelin in the numerous axons.

Bibliography

Books and Journals

Abbott, N.J. "Astrocyte-endothelial Interactions and Blood-brain Barrier Permeability." *Journal of Anatomy* 200 (2002): 629–638.

Alva, G., and S.G. Potkin. "Alzheimer's Disease and Other Dementias." *Clinics in Geriatric Medicine* 19 (2003): 763–776.

American Psychiatric Association. *Task Force on Tardive Dyskinesia*. Washington, D.C.: American Psychiatric Association, 1992.

Arzt, E., L. Kovalovsky, L. Müllerigaz, M. Costas, P. Plazas, D. Refojo, M. Páez-Pereda, J. Reul, G. Stalla, and F. Holsboer. "Functional Cross-talk among Cytokines, T-Cell Receptor, and Glucocorticoid Receptor Transcriptional Activity and Action." *Annals of the New York Academy of Sciences* 917 (2000): 672–677.

Berczi, I., and A. Szentivanyi. "The Immune-Neuroendocrine Circuitry." *Neuroimmune Biology Vol. 3: The Immune-Neuroendocrine Circuitry: History and Progress*, eds. I. Berczi and A. Szentivanyi. Boston: Elsevier, 2003, 561–592.

Bloom, F., C.A. Nelson, and A. Lazerson. *Brain, Mind, and Behavior*, 3rd ed. New York: Worth Publishers, 2001.

Bouret, S.G., S.J. Draper, and R.B. Simerly. "Formation of Projection Pathways from the Arcuate Nucleus of the Hypothalamus to Hypothalamic Regions Implicated in the Neural Control of Feeding Behavior in Mice." *Journal of Neuroscience* 24 (2004): 2797–2805.

Bowman, T. J. *Review of Sleep Medicine*. Boston: Butterworth Heinemann/Elsevier Science, 2003.

Broadbent, N.J., R.E. Clark, S. Zola, and L.R. Squire. "The Medial Temporal Lobe and Memory." *Neuropsychology of*

Memory, 3ʳᵈ ed., eds. L.R. Squire and D.L. Schacter. New York: The Guilford Press, 2002, 3–23.

Bruns, J., Jr., and W.A. Hauser. "The Epidemiology of Traumatic Brain Injury: A Review." *Epilepsia* 44 (Suppl. 10) (2003): 2–10.

Caplan, L.R., *Caplan's Stroke: A Clinical Approach*, 3ʳᵈ ed. Boston: Butterworth-Heinemann, 2000.

Carlson, N.R., *Physiology of Behavior*, 6ᵗʰ ed. Boston: Allyn and Bacon, 1998.

Carlson, N.R., *Physiology of Behavior*, 9ᵗʰ ed. Boston: Pearson Education, Inc., 2007.

Carlson, N.R., and W. Buskist. *Psychology: The Science of Behavior*, 5ᵗʰ ed. Boston: Allyn and Bacon, 1997.

Carper, J. *Your Miracle Brain*. New York: HarperCollins Publishers, 2000.

Castro, A.J., M.P. Merchut, E.J. Neafsey, and R.D. Wurster. *Neuroscience: An Outline Approach*. St. Louis, MO: Mosby Publishing, 2002.

Cheer, J.F., K.M. Wassum, M.L.A.V. Heien, P.E.M. Philips, and R.M. Wightman. "Cannaboids Enhance Subsecond Dopamine Release in the Nucleus Accumbens of Awake Rats." *The Journal of Neuroscience* 24 (2004): 4393–4400.

Chou, T.C., T.E. Scammell, J.J. Gooley, S.E. Gaus, C.B. Saper, and J. Lu. "Critical Role of Dorsomedial Hypothalamic Nucleus in a Wide Range of Behavioral Circadian Rhythms." *The Journal of Neuroscience* 23 (2003): 10691–10702.

Cooper, J.R., F.E. Bloom, and R.H. Roth. *The Biochemical Basis of Neuropharmacology*, 8ᵗʰ ed. New York: Oxford University Press, 2003.

D'Andrea, M.R. "Evidence Linking Neuronal Cell Death to Autoimmunity in Alzheimer's Disease." *Brain Research* 982 (2003): 19–30.

Doyon, J., and L.G. Ungerleider. "Functional Anatomy of Motor Skill Learning." *Neuropsychology of Memory*, 3ʳᵈ ed., eds. L.R. Squire and D.L. Schacter. New York: The Guilford Press, 2002, 225–238.

Duncan, J., and A.M. Owen. "Common Regions of the Human Frontal Lobe Recruited by Diverse Cognitive Demands." *Trends in Neurosciences* 23 (2000).

Ekdahl, C.T., J.H. Claasen, S. Bonde, Z. Kokaia, and O. Lindvall. "Inflammation Is Detrimental for Neurogenesis in Adult Brain." *Proceedings of the National Academy of Sciences, USA* 100 (2003): 13632–13637.

Finger, S. *Minds Behind the Brain: A History of the Pioneers and Their Discoveries.* Oxford: Oxford University Press, Inc., 2000.

Fitzgerald, M.J.T. *Neuroanatomy: Basic and Clinical*, 2nd ed. Philadelphia: Balliere Tindall, 1992.

FitzGerald, M.J.T., and J. Folan-Curran. *Clinical Neuroanatomy and Related Neuroscience*, 4th ed. New York: W.B. Saunders, 2002.

Florence, T.M. "Free Radicals in Parkinson's Disease." *Journal of Neurology* 249 (Suppl. 2) (2002): 1–5.

Frank, M.G., Benington, J.H. "The Role of Sleep in Memory Consolidation and Brain Plasticity: Dream or Reality?" *Neuroscientis* 12 (2006): 477–88.

Frey, L.C. "Epidemiology of Posttraumatic Epilepsy: A Critical Review." *Epilepsia* 44 (Suppl. 10) (2003): 11–17.

Gabry, K.E., G. Chrousos, and P.W. Gold. "The Hypothalamic-Pituitary-Adrenal (HPA) Axis: A Major Mediator of the Adaptive Responses to Stress." *Neuroimmune Biology Vol. 3: The Immune-Neuroendocrine Circuitry: History and Progress*, eds. I. Berczi and A. Szentivanyi. Boston: Elsevier, 2003.

Gazzaniga, M.D., R.B. Ivry, and G.R. Mangun. *Cognitive Neuroscience*, 2nd ed. New York: W.W. Norton and Company, 2002.

Gershberg, F.B., and A.P. Shimamura. "The Neuropsychology of Human Learning and Memory." *Neurobiology of*

Learning and Memory. San Diego: Academic Press, 1998, 33–359.

Gilman, S., and S.W. Newman. *Manter and Gatz's Essentials of Clinical Neuroanatomy and Neurophysiology,* 10th ed. Philadelphia: F.A. Davis Company, 1996.

Gleitman, H., A.J. Fridlund, and D. Reisberg. *Basic Psychology,* 5th ed. New York: W.W. Norton & Company, 2000.

Gluck, M.A., and C.E. Myers. "Psychobiological Models of Hippocampal Function in Learning and Memory." *Neurobiology of Learning and Memory.* San Diego: Academic Press, 1998, 417–448.

Gottwald, B., B. Wilde, Z. Mihajlovic, and H.M. Mehdorn. "Evidence for Distinct Cognitive Deficits After Focal Cerebellar Lesions." *Journal of Neurology, Neurosurgery, and Psychiatry* 75 (2004): 1524–1531.

Gray, P. *Psychology,* 3rd ed. New York: Worth Publishers, 1999.

Gronfier, C., and G. Brandenberger. "Ultradian Rhythms in Pituitary and Adrenal Hormones: Their Relations to Sleep." *Sleep Medicine Reviews* 2 (1998): 17–29.

Growdon, J.H., and N.R. Martin. *Blue Books of Practical Neurology: The Dementias.* Boston: Butterworth-Heinemann, 1998.

Hauser, W.A., and A. Pavone. "Introduction." *Epilepsia* 44 (Suppl. 10) (2003): 1.

Haines, D.E. *Fundamental Neuroscience.* Philadelphia: Churchill Livingstone, 2002.

Herd, J.A. "Cardiovascular Response to Stress." *Physiological Reviews* 71 (1991): 305–330.

Kennaway D.J., K. Lushington, D. Dawson, L. Lack, C. van den Heuvel, and N. Rogers. "Urinary 6-sulfatoxymelatonin Excretion and Aging: New Results and a Critical Review of the Literature." *Journal of Pineal Research* 27 (1999): 210–220.

Knowlton, B.J. "The Role of the Basal Ganglia in Learning and Memory." *Neuropsychology of Memory,* 3rd ed., eds. L.R.

Squire and D.L. Schacter. New York: The Guilford Press, 2002, 143–153.

Kolb, B., and I.Q. Whislaw. *An Introduction to Brain and Behavior.* New York: Worth Publishers, 2001.

Kolb, B., and I.Q. Whislaw. *An Introduction to Brain and Behavior.* 2nd ed. New York: Worth Publishers, 2006.

Koutsilieri, E., C. Scheller, E. Grunblatt, K. Nara, J. Li, and P. Riederer. "The Role of Free Radicals in Disease." *Australian and New Zealand Journal of Ophthamology* 23 (1995): 3–7.

Kuchler, M., K. Fouad, O. Weinmann, M.E. Schwab, and O. Raineteau. "Red Nucleus Projections to Distinct Motor Neuron Pools in the Rat Spinal Cord." *Journal of Comparative Neurology* 448 (2002): 349–359.

Launer, L.J. "Dietary Anti-Oxidants and the Risk for Brain Disease: The Hypothesis and Epidemiologic Evidence." *Diet-Brain Connection: Impact on Memory, Mood, Aging and Disease,* ed. M. P. Mattson. Boston: Kluwer Academic Publishers, 2002.

Lavie, P. "Sleep-Wake as a Biological Rhythm." *Annual Review of Psychology* 52 (2001): 277–303.

Li, C., P. Chen, and M.S. Smith. "Neuropeptide Y (NPY) Neurons in the Arcuate Nucleus (ARH) and Dorsomedial Nucleus (DMH), Areas Activated During Lactation, Project to the Paraventricular Nucleus of the Hypothalamus (PVH)." *Regulatory Peptides* 75 and 76 (1998): 93–100.

Mansvelder, H.D., M.D. Rover, D.S. McGehee, and A.B. Brussaard. "Cholinergic Modulation of Dopaminergic Reward Areas: Upstream and Downstream Targets of Nicotine Addiction." *European Journal of Pharmacology* 480 (2003): 117–123.

Martin, J.H. *Neuroanatomy: Text and Atlas,* 3rd ed. New York: McGraw-Hill Medical Publishing Division, 2003.

Martinez, J.L., Jr., E.J. Barea-Rodriguez, and B.E. Derrick. "Long-Term Potentiation, Long-Term Depression, and

Learning." *Neurobiology of Learning and Memory.* San Diego: Academic Press, 1998, 211–246.

Massion, J. "Red Nucleus: Past and Future." *Behavioral Brain Research* 28 (1988): 1–8.

McCurdy, M.L., D.I. Hansma, J.C. Houk, and A.R. Gibson. "Selective Projections from the Cat Red Nucleus to Digit Motor Neurons." *Journal of Comparative Neurology* 265 (1987): 367–379.

McGaugh, J.L. "The Amygdala Regulates Memory Consolidation." *Neuropsychology of Memory*, 3rd ed., eds. L.R. Squire and D.L. Schacter. New York: The Guilford Press, 2002, 437–449.

Mecocci, P. "Oxidative Stress in Mild Cognitive Impairment and Alzheimer's Disease: A Continuum. *Journal of Alzheimer's Disease* 6 (2004): 159–63.

Meythaler, J.M., J.D. Peduzzi, E. Eleftheriou, and T.A. Novack. "Current Concepts: Diffuse Axonal Injury-Associated Traumatic Brain Injury." *Archives of Physical Medicine and Rehabilitation* 82 (2001): 1461–1471.

Mulder, A.B., M.G. Hodenpijl, and F.H. Lopes da Silva. "Electrophysiology of the Hippocampal and Amygaloid Projections to the Nucleus Accumbens of the Rat: Convergence, Segregation, and Interaction of Inputs." Journal of Neuroscience (1998): 5095–6102.

Nance, D.M., and B.J. MacNeil. "Immunoregulation by Innervation. The Immune-Neuroendocrine Circuitry." *Neuroimmune Biology Vol 3: The Immune-Neuroendocrine Circuitry: History and Progress*, eds. I. Berczi and A. Szentivanyi. Boston: Elsevier, 2003.

Nathan, P.W., and M.C. Smith. "The Rubrospinal and Central Tegmental Tracts in Man." *Brain* 105 (Pt. 2) (1982): 223–269.

Nathans, J., T.P. Piantanida, R.L. Eddy, T.B. Shows, and D.S. Hogness. "Molecular Genetics of Inherited Variation in Human Color Vision." *Science* 232 (1986): 203–210.

Nestler, E.J. "Common Molecular and Cellular Substrates of Addiction and Memory." *Neurobiology of Learning and Memory* 78 (2002): 637–647.

———. "Total Recall—The Memory of Addiction." *Science* 292 (2001): 2266–2267.

Nolte, J. *The Human Brain: An Introduction to Its Functional Anatomy*, 5ᵗʰ ed. St. Louis: Mosby Publishing, 2002.

Oades, R.D., and G.M. Halliday. "Ventral Tegmental (A10) System: Neurobiology. 1. Anatomy and Connectivity." *Brain Research Reviews* (1987): 117–165.

Palkovits, M., and M. Fodor. "Distribution of Neuropeptides in the Human Lower Brainstem (Pons and Medulla Oblongata)." *Neurotransmitters in the Human Brain*, eds. D.J. Tracey et al. New York: Plenum Press, 1995, 101–113.

Pavone, P., R. Bianchini, E. Parano, G. Incorpora, R. Rizzo, L. Mazzone, and R.R. Trifiletti. "Anti-brain Antibodies in PANDAS Versus Uncomplicated Streptococcal Infection." *Pediatric Neurology* 30 (2004): 107–110.

Pinel, J.P.J. *Biopsychology*, 6ᵗʰ ed. Boston: Pearson Education, Inc., 2006.

Roitt, I., J. Brostoff, and D. Male. *Immunology*, 5ᵗʰ ed. Philadelphia: Mosby, 1998.

Rolls, E.T. "Memory Systems in the Brain." *Annual Review of Psychology* 51 (2000): 599–630.

Russo, E. "Controversy Surrounds Memory Mechanism." *The Scientist* 13 (1999): 1.

Shneerson, J.M. *Handbook of Sleep Medicine*. Malden, MA: Blackwell Science Ltd., 2000.

Snell, R.S. *Clinical Neuroanatomy: An Illustrated Review with Questions and Explanations*, 3ʳᵈ ed. Philadelphia: Lippincott, Williams & Wilkins, 2001.

Song, C., and B.E. Leonard. *Fundamentals of Psychoneuroimmunology*. New York: John Wiley & Sons, 2000.

Sullivan, E.V., and L. Marsh. "Hippocampal Volume Deficits in Alcoholic Korsakoff's Syndrome." *Neurology* 61 (2003): 1716–1719.

Swaab, D.F. *Handbook of Clinical Neurology Vol. 80* (3rd Series, Vol. 2). *The Human Hypothalamus: Basic and Clinical Aspects, Part I: Nuclei of the Human Hypothalamus.* Boston: Elsevier, 2004.

———. *Handbook of Clinical Neurology,* Vol. 80 (3rd Series, Vol. 2) *The Human Hypothalamus: Basic and Clinical Aspects, Part II: Neuropathology of the Human Hypothalamus and Adjacent Structures.* Boston: Elsevier, 2004.

Thompson, R.H., N.S. Canteras, and L.W. Swanson. "Organization of Projections from the Dorsomedial Nucleus of the Hypothalamus: A PHA-L Study in the Rat." *Journal of Comparative Neurology* 376 (1996): 143–173.

Usuda, I., K. Tanaka, and T. Chiba. "Efferent Projections of the Nucleus Accumbens in the Rat with Special Reference to Subdivision of the Nucleus: Biotinylated Dextran Amine Study." *Brain Research* (1998): 73–93.

Wagner, U., and J. Born. "Memory consolidation during sleep: Interactive effects of sleep stages and HPA regulation." *Stress* (2007).

Waxman, S.G. *Clinical Neuroanatomy.* New York: Lange Medical Books, 2003.

White, N.M. "Addictive Drugs as Reinforcers: Multiple Partial Actions on Memory Systems." *Addiction* 91 (1996): 921–949.

Wise, R.A. "Drug-activation of Brain Reward Pathways." *Drug and Alcohol Dependence* 51 (1998): 13–22.

Wolf, M.E. "Addiction: Making the Connection Between Behavioral Changes and Neuronal Plasticity in Specific Pathways." *Molecular Interventions* 2 (2002): 146–157.

Web Sites

The Anatomy of a Head Injury
http://www.ahs.uwaterloo.ca/~cahr/headfall.htm

Autoimmune Disease Research Center at the Johns Hopkins Medical Institution
http://autoimmune.pathology.jhmi.edu/

Autoimmune Disease Research Foundation

www.cureautoimmunity.org/Science%20release.htm

B.F. Skinner

http://www.ship.edu/~cgboeree/skinner.html

The Brain & the Actions of Cocaine, Opiates, and Marijuana

http://www.udel.edu/skeen/BB/Hpages Reward%20&%20Addiction2/actions.html

Brain Facts and Figures

http://faculty.washington.edu/chudler/facts.html

Brief Biography of B.F. Skinner

http://www.bfskinner.org/bio.asp

Can Christopher Reeve Get Off the Ventilator?

http://www.pulmonaryreviews.com/jan03/pr_jan03_superman.html

Caudate Nucleus

http://en.wikipedia.org/wiki/Caudate_nucleus

CDC: Fetal Alcohol Syndrome

http://www.cdc.gov/ncbddd/fas/default.htm

Cerebral Ventricular System and Cerebrospinal Fluid

http://www.umanitoba ca/faculties/medicine/anatomy/cv.htm

Chemical Warfare Primer

http://www.mnpoison.org/index.asp?pageID=146

Chemical Weapons: Nerve Agents

http://faculty.washington.edu/chudler/weap.html

Christopher Reeve Paralysis Foundation

http://www.christopherreeve.org

Cocaine Addiction Linked to a Glutamate Receptor

http://www.biomedcentral.com/news/20010829/04/

Cognitive Rehabilitation: What Is It?

http://cogrehab.home.pipeline.com/cogrehab.htm

Conditioned Emotional Reactions

http://psychclassics.yorku.ca/Watson/emotion.htm

The Ear

http://medic.med.uth.tmc.edu/Lecture/Main/ear.htm

Embryological Development of the Human Brain

www.newhorizons.org/neuro/scheibel.htm

The Enteric Nervous System

http://arbl.cvmbs.colostate.edu/hbooks/pathphys/digestion/
basics/gi_nervous.html

The Enteric Nervous System: A Second Brain

http://www.hosppract.com/issues/1999/07/gershon.htm

The Eye

http://medocs.ucdavis.edu/cha/402/lectsyl/98/eye.HTM

Feuerstein's Instrumental Enrichment Program: Basic Theory

http://www.icelp.org/asp/Basic_Theory.shtm

Free Radicals and Human Disease

http://www.drproctor.com/crcpap2.htm

From Neurobiology to Treatment: Progress Against Addiction

http://www.nature.com/cgi-taf/DynaPage.taf?file=/neuro/
journal/v5/n11s/full/nn945.htmlUT

The Functions of Glia – An Overview

http://www.abcam.com/index.
html?pageconfig=resource&rid=10596&pid=7

Gulf War Syndrome Research Reveals Present Danger

http://www.newscientist.com/news/news.
jsp?id=ns99993546

How CAT Scans Work

http://science.howstuffworks.com/cat-scan.htm

How MRI Works

http://electronics.howstuffworks.com/mri.htm

The Internet Stroke Center: About Stroke

http://www.strokecenter.org/pat/about.htm

Is Mercury Toxicity an Autoimmune Disorder?

http://www.thorne.com/townsend/oct/mercury.html

Korsakoff's Syndrome

http://www.chclibrary.org/micromed/00054130.html

The Mayo Clinic: Spinal Cord Injury

http://www.mayoclinic.com/invoke.cfm?id=DS00460

Mechanoreceptors Specialized to Receive Tactile Information

http://www.ncbi.nlm.nih.gov/books/bv.fcgi?rid=neurosci.section.615

Medline Plus: Taste—Impaired

http://www.nlm.nih.gov/medlineplus/ency/article/003050.htm

Medline Plus: Spinal Cord Injuries

http://www.nlm.nih.gov/medlineplus/spinalcordinjuries.html

Melatonin: A Review

http://www.priory.com/mel.htm

Melatonin Information and References

http://www.aeiveos.com/diet/melatonin/

The Meninges and Cerebrospinal Fluid

http://www.csuchico.edu/~pmccaffrey//syllabi/CMSD%20320/362unit3.html

Modulation of Prefrontal Cortex (PFC) and Fusiform Face Area (FFA) Responses to Increased Working Memory Demand for Faces

http://www.uchsc.edu/sm/mstp/aspen99/html/oralhtml/oral_Druzgal_J.html

Monell Chemical Senses

http://www.monell.org/

MS Information Sourcebook

http://www.nationalmssociety.org/Sourcebook.asp

Nathaniel Kleitman (1895–1999)

http://www.uchospitals.edu/news/1999/
19990816-kleitman.php

Neuroanatomy and Physiology of the "Brain Reward System" in Substance Abuse

http://ibgwww.colorado.edu/cadd/a_drug/essays/
essay4.htm

Neuroembriology

http://www.humanneurophysiology.com/
neuroembriology.htm

Neurons, Synapses, Action Potentials, and Neurotransmission

http://www.mind.ilstu.edu/curriculum/neurons_intro/neu-
rons_intro.php

Neurotransmitter Systems I

http://artsci-ccwin.concordia.ca/psychology/psyc358/Lec-
tures/transmit1.htm

NINDS: Neurological Disorders and Disease Index

*http://www.ninds.nih.gov/health_and_medical/disorder_*
index.htm

Oral Cavity and Teeth

http://medic.med.uth.tmc.edu/Lecture/Main/tool2.htm

Overview of Hypothalamic and Pituitary Hormones

http://arbl.cvmbs.colostate.edu/hbooks/pathphys/endo-
crine/hypopit/overview.html

Parasomnias (Sleep Walking, Sleep Talking, and Sleep Eating)

http://www.sleepdoctor.com/sw_st.htm

Pathophysiology of AD: Free Radicals

*http://www.alzheimersdisease.com/hcp/about/patho/hcp_
free_radicals.jsp?checked=y*

Patient H.M.

http://www.psy.ohio-state.edu/psy312/deniz-hm.html

The Phineas Gage Information Page

http://www.deakin.edu.au/hbs/GAGEPAGE

The Physiology of Taste

*http://www.sff.net/people/mberry/taste.htmPrion Diseases
and the BSE Crisis*

Pick's Disease Pathology: Pick Bodies

http://www.binderlab.northwestern.edu/pickbodies.html

The Pleasure Centres Affected by Drugs

*http://www.thebrain.mcgill.ca/flash/i/i_03/i_03_cr/i_03_
cr_par/i_03_cr_par.html*

Prion Diseases and the BSE Crisis

http://www.sciencemag.org/feature/data/prusiner/245.shl

The Prion Theory

*http://www.portfolio.mvm.ed.ac.uk/studentwebs/session2/
group4/evidence.htm*

The Role of Sleep in Memory

*http://www.memory-key.com/NatureofMemory/sleep_
news.htm*

Simple Anatomy of the Retina

http://webvision.med.utah.edu/sretina.html

Sleep and Language

http://thalamus.wustl.edu/course/sleep.html

Sleep Deprivation

*http://www.macalester.edu/~psych/whathap/UBNRP/
sleep_deprivation/titlepage.html*

Smell and Taste Disorders

http://www.entnet.org/healthinfo/topics/smell_taste.cfm

Southwestern's Eric J. Nestler on the Molecular Biology of Addiction

http://www.sciencewatch.com/nov-dec2001/sw_nov-dec2001_page3.htm

Skeletal Development in Humans: A Model for the Study of Developmental Genes

http://www.infobiogen.fr/services/chromcancer/IntroItems/GenDevelLongEngl.html

Spinal Cord Injury Facts & Statistics

http://www.sci-info-pages.com/facts.html

SPINALCORD: Spinal Cord Injury Information Network

http://www.spinalcord.uab.edu

The Stages of Sleep

http://www.silentpartners.org/sleep/sinfo/s101/physio4.htm

The Strange Tale of Phineas Gage

http://www.brainconnection.com/topics/?main=fa/phineas-gage

Stress

http://www.neuroanatomy.wisc.edu/coursebook/neuro4(2).pdf

Stroke Statistics

http://www.strokecenter.org/patients/stats.htm

Substances of Abuse and Addiction

http://abdellab.sunderland.ac.uk/lectures/addiction/opiates1.html

Tardive Dyskinesia/Tardive Dystonia

http://www.breggin.com/tardivedysk.html

Taste—A Brief Tutorial by Tim Jacob

http://www.cf.ac.uk/biosi/staff/jacob/teaching/sensory/taste.html

That's Tasty
http://faculty.washington.edu/chudler/tasty.html

Toxicity, Organophosphates
http://www.emedicine.com/ped/topic1660.htm

Transport Across Cell Membranes
*http://users.rcn.com/jkimball.ma.ultranet/BiologyPages/D/
Diffusion.html*

**Traumatic Brain Injury: Definition, Epidemiology,
Pathophysiology**
http://www.emedicine.com/pmr/topic212.htm

Vagus Nerve
*http://www.meddean.luc.edu/lumen/MedEd/
grossAnatomy/h_n/cn/cn1/cn10.htm*

What Is the Function of the Various Brain Waves?
http://brain.web-us.com/brainwavesfunction.htm

What Is Traumatic Brain Injury?
http://www.cdc.gov/ncipc/tbi/TBI.htm

Further Resources

Books and Journals

Alzheimer's Disease: Unraveling the Mystery. National Institute on Aging, National Institutes of Health Publication No. 02-3782, October 2002.

Blaylock, R.L. *Excitotoxins: The Taste That Kills.* Santa Fe: Health Press, 1997.

Bowman, J.P., and F.D. Giddings. *Strokes: An Illustrated Guide to Brain Structure, Blood Supply, and Clinical Signs.* Upper Saddle River, NJ: Prentice Hall, 2003.

Carper, J. *Your Miracle Brain.* New York: HarperCollins Publishers, 2000.

Hoffer, A., and M. Walker. *Smart Nutrients: Prevent and Treat Alzheimer's, Enhance Brain Function.* Garden City, NY: Morton Walker, 1994.

Holford, P. *Optimum Nutrition for the Mind.* London: Piatkus Books, 2007.

Matthews, G.G. *Introduction to Neuroscience (11th Hour).* Malden, MA: Blackwell Science, Inc., 2000.

McEwen, B.S., with E.N. Lasley. *The End of Stress As We Know It.* Washington, D.C.: Joseph Henry Press, 2002.

Nowinski, C. *Head Games: Football's Concussion Crisis.* East Bridgewater, MA: The Drummond Publishing Group, 2007.

Null, G. *Mind Power.* New York: New American Library, 2005.

Osborn, C.L. *Over My Head: A Doctor's Own Story of Head Injury from the Inside Looking Out.* Andrews McMeel Publishers, 1998.

Philpott, W.P., and D.K. Kalita. *Brain Allergies.* Los Angeles: Keats Publications, 2000.

Rolls, E.T. "Memory Systems in the Brain." *Annual Review of Psychology* 51 (2000): 599–630.

Springer, S.P., and G. Deutsch. *Left Brain, Right Brain: Perspectives from Cognitive Neuroscience*, 5th ed. New York: W. H. Freeman and Company, 1998.

Walker, S. III. *A Dose of Sanity*. New York City: John Wiley & Sons, 1997.

Whalley, L. *The Aging Brain*. New York: Columbia University Press, 2001.

Woolsey, T.A., J. Hanaway, and M.H. Gado. *The Brain Atlas: A Visual Guide to the Human Central Nervous System*. New York: Wiley-Liss, 2002.

Web Sites

Animated Tutorials: Neurobiology/Biopsychology
http://www.sumanasinc.com/webcontent/anisamples/neurobiology/neurobiology.html

The Brain
http://www.enchantedlearning.com/subjects/anatomy/brain/index.shtml

BrainMaps.org
http://brainmaps.org/index.php

A Brief Introduction to the Brain
http://ifcsun1.ifisiol.unam.mx/Brain/segunda.htm

Brain Connection
http://www.brainconnection.com/

BrainMind.com (Interactive Functional Brain Maps)
http://brainmind.com/BrainMaps5.html

BrainSource.com
http://www.brainsource.com/

Brain Web
http://www.dana.org/brainweb/

Brain Work
http://www.dana.org/books/press/brainwork/

Central Nervous System: Visual Perspectives
http://3d-brain.ki.se/index.html

Dana.org
http://www.dana.org

Explore the Brain and Spinal Cord
http://faculty.washington.edu/chudler/introb.html

The HOPES Brain Tutorial
http://www.stanford.edu/group/hopes/basics/
braintut/ab1.html

How Your Brain Works
http://science.howstuffworks.com/brain.htm

NeuralLinks Plus
http://spot.colorado.edu/~dubin/bookmarks/index.html

Neuroanatomy Lab Resource Appendices—Sectional Atlas
http://isc.temple.edu/neuroanatomy/lab/atlas/msc/

Neuroscience
http://cte.rockhurst.edu/neuroscience/page/outline.shtml

Neuroscience: A Journey Through the Brain
http://ntsrv2000.educ.ualberta.ca/nethowto/examples/
edit435/M_davies/Neuroscience%20Web/index.htm#

Neuroscience Education
http://faculty.washington.edu/chudler/ehceduc.html

Neuroscience Tutorial
http://thalamus.wustl.edu/course

Milestones in Neuroscience Research
http://www.univ.trieste.it/~brain/NeuroBiol/Neuroscienze
%20per%20tutti/hist.html

Neuroscience Links
http://www.iespana.es/neurociencias/links.htm

Picture Credits

Page

13: © Infobase Publishing
15: © Infobase Publishing
20: © Infobase Publishing
21: © Infobase Publishing
24: © Infobase Publishing
27: © Infobase Publishing
28: © Infobase Publishing
36: © Infobase Publishing
38: © Infobase Publishing
45: © Infobase Publishing
46: © Infobase Publishing
61: © Infobase Publishing
65: © Infobase Publishing
67: © Infobase Publishing
72: © Infobase Publishing
75: © Infobase Publishing
83: © Infobase Publishing
84: © Infobase Publishing
89: © Infobase Publishing
91: © Infobase Publishing
102: © Infobase Publishing
104: © Infobase Publishing
106: © Infobase Publishing
108: © Infobase Publishing
117: © Infobase Publishing
123: © Infobase Publishing
128: © Infobase Publishing
140: © Infobase Publishing
143: © Infobase Publishing
146: © Infobase Publishing
155: © Infobase Publishing
159: © Infobase Publishing
167: Roger Ressmeyer/
     CORBIS

Index